Cinderella Was a Liar

Cinderella Was a Liar

The Real Reason
You Can't
Find (or Keep)
a Prince

Brenda Della Casa

McGraw
Graw
Hill

New York Chicago San Francisco Lisbon London Madrid Mexico City
Milan New Delhi San Juan Seoul Singapore Sydney Toronto

The McGraw·Hill Companies

Library of Congress Cataloging-in-Publication Data

Della Casa, Brenda.
   Cinderella was a liar : the real reason you can't find (or keep) a prince / by Brenda
Della Casa.
      p.   cm.
   ISBN 0-07-147653-9 (alk. paper)
   1. Dating (Social customs)   I. Title.

HQ801.D452   2007
306.73—dc22   2006026814

1 2 3 4 5 6 7 8 9 10 11 12 13 14 15 16   FGR/FGR   0 9 8 7 6

ISBN-13: 978-0-07-147653-9
ISBN-10:   0-07-147653-9

Interior design by Bartko Design Inc.

McGraw-Hill books are available at special quantity discounts to use as premiums and
sales promotions, or for use in corporate training programs. For more information, please
write to the Director of Special Sales, Professional Publishing, McGraw-Hill, Two Penn
Plaza, New York, NY 10121-2298. Or contact your local bookstore.

This book is printed on acid-free paper.

This book is dedicated to my beloved grandfather Mancie Herring and my great-aunt Sibyl Ereaux. Everything that is good in me stems from your love and teachings. I know you are watching above me from heaven, and my only goal in life is to make you proud. I shall speak your names every day, and you shall live in my heart forever. Thank you for my only experiences with unconditional love. It was magical.

Contents

Acknowledgments

ONE'S ACCOMPLISHMENTS in life are usually made possible with the help, love, encouragement, and support of those around them, and I am no exception. While I cannot thank every person who has ever meant something to me or been there for me, I hope I let those who have know how much they are appreciated through my actions toward them every day.

The biggest thank-you goes to the many men and women who allowed me to interview them for this book—for filling out long questionnaires, sitting through the discussions, trusting me with their experiences, and allowing me to share their quotes.

Special thanks to Charlie DeMarco and my Phat Phree Phamily for keeping me on my toes, encouraging me to be the best writer I can be, nurturing my sense of humor, and being the great, loyal, and hilarious team they are. Thanks to posters Christine, Atlas, Deuce, and Tom A.

I would like to thank my agent, Byrd Leavell, for all of his help, encouragement, and support through this whole process (thanks for the therapy sessions!). Thanks to my amazing editor, mentor, and friend, Natasha Graf, for going above and beyond for this book. Thank you to Deb Brody for putting up with my worries and questions and for taking me under her wing and believing in my work. You are supremely talented. Thank you so much to Michele Matrisciani for believing in me and this book and for fighting so hard. Thanks to Sarah Love. You are the best; thank you for everything! To Susan Moore—thank you for your kindness and enthusiasm. Thanks to Ann Pryor; you are amazing. Thanks to Eric Trenkamp for his patience and making me look and sound good.

I would like to give a big hug and thank-you to Sharon Ecke for all of her support and encouragement (and for introducing me to the Phat Phree!). Thanks to Cari Wira-Dineen for going above and beyond to help make my dreams of living as a writer a reality. Thank you to *For Me* magazine for giving me my start.

Thank you to Sonya Funna, GMFT, for her insight and many IM sessions.

To Marty Pritikin—you knew the scared girl I was and helped make me the woman I am today. You are a gift in my life, and I love you dearly. I finally made it to the starting line! I love you, dude.

A huge thank-you to my amazing family of friends who have helped me through this process: Marc Dare (Good Vibes, Frankie, I truly love you); Jeffrey Simon; Yinh Hinh (you are the Hope Diamond of friends); Kris Abdelmessih (Muppet Man, you're just awesome); "My Daisy" Barbara Reinhard; David Dineen (you're the real deal); Mark Lewis; Lukshmi Puttanniah; Joanna Riverra; Ben Dean; Frank Sibillo; Auntie Rosa and Uncle Joe (you surpass most people in many ways; thank you for being so supportive and interesting); my sisters (you can do and be anything; never forget that); Dominique Prunetti; Brian Goldberg; Robert Mazza (Big Daddy, I love you!); Naomi Ben-Or; Louisa Griffith-Jones; Maria Antoniou; Julie Stone for her constant brainstorming and support—you are as dedicated to this book as I am, and I love you for it! Thank you to Matt Hutchinson and to the Ganz sisters, Debbie and Lisa.

A special thank-you to Christine Seddon for all of her love and support in this process and in my life. Thanks for sharing your thoughts, ears, and dating stories on a daily basis. Many thanks to my super-doggies Tony and Baron for letting me read aloud to them every day!

A big hug to Vance DeGeneres for spending hours online promising me this book would meet my expectations and for the constant laughs. You are a real talent.

I would also like to thank the following people for their assistance, love, and support through my life and this project: President Clinton for giving me the encouragement to follow my dreams and to never give up, American University, Jen and the Smolen Family (I will always love and appreciate every one of you), Rosa Soper, Ian Soper, the Bella Vista High School staff for literally replacing my missing family and raising me, and the countless people and families who opened their homes to me to ensure I had food to eat and a warm bed to sleep in.

I will close by thanking my partner, closest friend, and amazing source of laughter and unshakable love, Harold Soper. You walk beside me and make every day a journey with the brightest of possibilities. I look forward to spending the rest of my days knocking over goals and experiencing and enjoying life with you. Thank you for all of the hours of allowing me to interview you and for your honesty and candor in this process and life. I love you more than you will ever know, Mono!

There are so many others who have blessed my life. Thank you.

Introduction

RECENTLY MY GIRLFRIENDS and I uncorked several bottles of wine, sat back, and shared our deepest secrets, best advice, and most candid opinions about men, love, dating, and relationships. We were having quite the little pity-party when it occurred to me that we were all complaining about the same thing: no man was living up to our sky-high ideals. Not even the "good" ones. "Where in the hell is my prince?" my girlfriend yelled. We all laughed, but then the room fell silent, and soon the smiles faded.

It was a question we'd been asking ourselves since we first got that woozy feeling when our favorite boy walked by in grade school. And here we were, in our late twenties and thirties, still waiting for answers to come trotting in on a beautiful, white stallion.

The Fairy Tale That Started It All

So, where in the heck did this fascination with the ultimate romance come from anyway? When did we start believing in the idea of a perfect man who would swoop into our lives and eliminate the negatives? Well, for me it was at the age of four when my great-aunt Vyvian introduced me to a saucy chick by the name of Cinderella.

From the first time I heard the tale of the sweet, docile little stepchild with the kind heart whose prince saved her from her nasty stepfamily, it was my favorite. How could it not be?

The ending was the happiest I had ever heard! From then on, I wanted to be exactly like my favorite maiden, and judging from the countless princess costumes I saw on Halloween, I was not alone in my desire for a life in a castle alongside a handsome royal.

These days, it is safe to assume that almost every maiden between the ages of five and ninety-five has heard one of the 340 different versions of the tale that has been encouraging daydreams (and disappointing single women, wives, and girlfriends) since the ninth century. While the details in each rendition may vary (e.g., gold slippers vs. glass ones, a magical fish instead of a fairy godmother), the promise of the plot remains the same: good girls with tender hearts and big wishes will not only be given a chance to attend the ball, but they'll beat out all of the other lonely maidens and meet a perfect prince who will change their lives and love them forever.

And unlike some blue bloods we've seen, your prince will not be a stuffy, scrawny guy with large ears. No way! Yours will be a supremely hot hunk of a man, a charismatic fellow with a knack for romance who is totally void of any of the flaws that will cause you frustration or disappointment. Cinderella promised us a prince who will not be annoyed or exhausted by our issues. Instead he will be willing, eager, and able to remove any unhappiness from your life by carrying you straight to your happily ever after. This is a place where there are no tears, no Xbox obsessions, no secret porn collections, and no arguments about how to leave the toilet seat once finished.

Now, if you are anything like the rest of us, you know that by the standards set here in the real world, Cinderella was one lucky chick. Still, even with daily proof that this perfect love story is an uncommon one, we just can't seem to stop ourselves from allowing our wish for that kind of fairy-tale courtship to invade our thoughts (and cause us to eat more than a few servings of Chunky Monkey and down one too many mojitos) more often than we'd ever admit to one another.

Face it, gals: most of us are a bunch of romance junkies, and Cinderella gave us our first hit.

But Where the Hell Is He?

Just as our favorite princess's promise has stood the test of time, so has every maiden's hope that a hero will save her from a life of dessert for one. We are all searching for Prince Wonderful, and some of us are willing to risk our reputations and bet our hearts on a stranger to find him. With women lining up and pouring their hearts out on casting tapes for a chance to be on romantic reality shows such as "The Bachelor," and others e-mailing *Cosmopolitan* magazine's "50 Most Eligible Bachelors," one thing is clear: the desire to slip on that special stiletto is as strong today as it was centuries ago when Cinderella first shared her tale.

We're under the impression that there is a terrible shortage of worthy royals these days (which is totally not true, by the way, but more on that later). The older we become and the more toads we date, the less likely we are to believe that any regular lad could possibly live up to the ideal standard set by the one Cinderella claims she snagged.

Notice that I didn't say we did not believe in the ideal; we just didn't believe that any of the guys we met could live up to it. This distinction can cause quite a bit of disappointment for both sides. We're thinking our partners should be heroes, and instead our partners are being punished or cast aside for being human. The sad truth is that most maidens are comparing every man they meet to the gorgeous royal with the admirable capability to whitewash their lives with a kiss. He holds the key to every heart in the land.

Alas, after kissing more than your fair share of toads, you now know that the prince we daydream about is an elusive soul. Furthermore, no self-respecting female would ever leave her shoe behind after meeting him, thank you!

Cinderella Was a Liar

The reality is that no matter how independent a maiden you are, flying solo is no fairy tale, and even if you do get the slipper, there are no guarantees. No matter how beautiful your dress, how sexy your perfume, or how tender your heart is most of the time, Prince Wonderful does not pay you a visit by climbing up your balcony. *Hell, he doesn't even call.*

If you have ever sat in front of the television on a Friday night wondering, "What in the hell happened to the fairy tale? Where's my happily ever after?" then it's time you knew the truth: Cinderella was a liar.

In her tale of easy love, she omitted the realities of her situation and screwed every maiden who ever heard her story by giving them unrealistic expectations and a flawed blueprint.

This fact is not pleasant, but it leaves us with two options:

1. We can all sit here and whine about the cuts caused by broken glass slippers.
2. We can change out of our single-in-distress garb and move past the fairy tale.

If you choose the latter, you're in for quite a journey as we are about to uncover the real way to get the new and attainable happy ending instead of that unrealistic fantasy you were promised.

The Secrets That Will Be Shared in This Book

I have come up with the answers you are all looking for in a variety of ways. First, working as a casting producer and recruiter for dozens of relationship shows has given me a unique opportunity to immerse myself into the singles scene and to interview literally thousands of single men and women with a variety of backgrounds, desires, experiences, and viewpoints. Working as a magazine writer and journalist has offered me a chance to interview top relationship experts and dozens of singles to find out what makes a relationship work, what doesn't, and what will send a man packing.

This brings me to the research done specifically for this book. Hundreds of single, married, and divorced men from around the world were asked to answer specific questions asked by women during a variety of interviews and roundtable discussions. The great thing is these men didn't hold back, but the bad news is that most of the women in the dating scene have got it all wrong! (Please note: the names and identifying information of these men have been changed in exchange for complete disclosure.)

I am about to share with you all of the juicy tidbits as to what makes a man *want* to be exclusive, what will ruin your chances with him even when he's hooked, and how they really feel about games and all of your overanalyzing. You're going to find out the truth about what these men look for in a girl-friend and wife, what will make them run for the hills, and the truth about one-night stands. Through direct quotes, you will read their viewpoints about love, sex, cheating, and their idea of what a date really means. I plan to share it all with you, but to do that, you are going to have to look into the mirror and be prepared to hear everything it has to say.

Cinderella Was a Liar is all about accepting your reality, and it isn't that all men are toads or that you are destined to be alone. You'll learn to accept that men are not afraid of commitment any more than women are and to accept that every handsome suitor you meet won't be carrying a slipper in your size. You'll see that, here in the real world, princes are all around you, but because you may be so fixated on your own idea of perfection, you haven't even noticed their charm. In addition, just because you don't currently have a lad to call your own doesn't mean you have not met *several* royal babes with the potential of showing you a ball. You might be completely covered in warts from all the toads you've been kissing, but the only way to get to the happy ending is to start from the very beginning and figure out where we have been going wrong.

Yes, I said "we." It's time we stop telling ourselves that the world is full of toads and accepting that fantastic lads are simply "not into us." It's time to find out why.

In the coming chapters, you are going to have a chance to peek into the crystal ball and identify what it is that you have been doing to prevent yourself from having the romantic life you want and deserve. You will start to understand that you have to date yourself before you'll ever be a great date to anyone else. Whether your feet are covered with blisters from wearing slippers that don't fit, you have been holing up with a toad who doesn't deserve you, or you have been punishing yourself for being single, it's all going to change—right now.

You're about to learn some simple dating magic: change your actions, reactions, expectations, and outlook, and you'll have better luck in your relationships with not only men but also with everyone in your life—and most important, yourself!

So, are you ready to rewrite the fairy tale?

Yes? Great, let's do it!

Chapter 1

---•---

The Twelve Sisters
No Prince Wants to Date

NCE UPON A time in a land not so far away, you spent a Saturday night on the town with your best girlfriends. You met a supersexy, wonderful lad who swept you off of your feet and sent your heart aflutter at first glance. Smart and sophisticated, this dreamboat was both handsome and interesting, and above all, he was totally enchanted by you! How could he not be? You were wearing your sexy new jeans and had your A-game going strong. The fact is, you were utterly irresistible, and he was flickering around you like a moth to a flame.

As the evening progressed, the conversation flowed effortlessly as the barmaid poured wine into your goblets. By the end of the evening he made it clear that he wanted to see you again. Soon. Very soon. You excitedly exchanged phone numbers and several sweet good-nights.

Not long after you hopped in your carriage/car/cab, you caught yourself pinching your arm a little just to make sure it was not all a dream. You were sure you had just met a prince, and your night with your new Mr. Wonderful left you with the feeling that you were floating, *as though you were living in a fairy tale.*

The next day, you told all of your girlfriends, coworkers, and anyone else who would listen all about this sensational new suitor and caught yourself daydreaming about what a relationship with him might be like. You wondered, Where did he live? What was his mother like? What would it be like to kiss him? The more you fantasized about him, the more excited you became. You could not wait to get to know him better or, better yet, for him to get to know you!

When your big night arrived, you left nothing to chance. With your fairy godmother indisposed, you relied on the magic of your nearly maxed-out Platinum Dust card and bought the hottest little black ball gown you could find. You got a blowout and dabbed your sauciest oils in all of the right places (wink). Just as you were starting to get a little anxious, your new could-be-prince picked you up, and off you went.

The date started off well with chemistry igniting small fires between you, but then something went terribly awry. Somewhere between drinks and the good-night peck on the cheek you decided he might be "the One," and he decided he would not be calling you again—ever.

Ouch. Welcome to the real world of dating, where there are no magic aids, no granted wishes, and very few second chances.

What Happened? Did You Scare Him Away?

Now, sometimes things just don't click, and that is OK; we've all walked home with a pumpkin in tow. But what about those times when things are clicking faster and louder than your

Stuart Weitzmans on wet concrete, and then, **BOOM**, he's dropping you off and avoiding you at parties?

Well, darling, somewhere along the date you scared your wonderful suitor away.

"However did I do that?" you ask.

Well, it's simple; he could have very well been the blue blood carrying a slipper in your size, but you'll never know it because something you did or said made him think you were more frightening than fabulous.

Now, before you start getting defensive and tell me what a catch you are and start explaining that he clearly misunderstood you, understand that I am not one of your girlfriends. I am not going to sit here and help you convince yourself that he was a bad guy and it was his loss, because that wasn't the case; and, if it was, that's not the case most of the time. That kind of ego stroking is not going to get you anywhere except where you are right now—alone and wondering why you can't keep a lad interested.

I am sure you are a fantastic maiden, but I am also sure that you have a bunch of quirks you are completely unaware of or refuse to acknowledge, which is why you bought this book. Somewhere, deep down, you know that you need to change. Now, don't get all distraught; you've got to know that we have all given off the wrong impression and blown it with someone, whether it was a suitor, a potential boss, or a random person on the street. No one is perfect, and as much as I hate to admit it (and risk many friendships by doing so), every maiden I know— including myself—has acted like one of the following sisters. The great thing is you have all of the power here, as everything you don't like about your dating life can change once you hold yourself accountable, stop wishing for a prince to swoop in out of nowhere, and commit yourself to changing your own bad behavior—instead of candy coating it to make your solo status easier to swallow.

So, before you allow yet another lovely night to be ruined by an ugly habit you cannot pinpoint or act in a manner that sends the wrong message, take a look here and read all about the twelve sisters no prince wants to date.

Number One: The Desperate Sister

Someone throw this gal a lifeline before she drowns in her desire to be matched up! The desperate maiden despises everything about living for one, and she's willing to date just about anyone to be able to order in for two. How do we know? Because every verbal path leads to the draining conversation where she whines about not having someone, notes that all of the ladies in her circle have met someone, and wonders aloud why she can't even get anyone to call her back. This maiden wants a boyfriend more than anything else in the world, including a solid partner. Any old lad will do, and her yearning just seeps out of her pores like garlic. It's pungent and unattractive.

Are You Fighting the Dragon of Desperation?

No gal wants to admit she's gone the way of desperation, but before you kid yourself any further, take a moment to do a checkup. The reality is that if you find yourself dating or, worse, *sleeping with* men you are not attracted to, then you, my dear, are none other than *le desperate mademoiselle.* Do you find yourself putting up with disrespectful or hurtful behavior because you believe the power of your love can magically transform a toad into your prince?

Yup, you're kidding yourself. If nights out have become a mission, you are harassing your friends to set you up with their recently divorced neighbor, or you've spent a Tuesday night searching all of the lads eighty and under on AnyOldToad .com, there might be an issue. If your biological clock ticks so loud that it interrupts conversation and men are running away thinking it's the sound of a time bomb about to explode, it's time to pull out the Neosporin and medicate the skin you've scratched off of your ring finger. Put simply: it's time to chill out and gain a little perspective.

Why Changing Will Work in the Long Run

Fantasizing about a boyfriend changing your life the way most people do about winning the lottery means that it is high time to cash in that reality check. By pretending to have things in common with every lad you meet or measuring your self-esteem against the ideal "partnered you," you are setting yourself up for heartbreak and disappointment every day you don't meet your prince.

It is a sad fact that desperate maidens rarely get the crown because they are usually somewhere else, settling for the first toad that shows a little interest. These gals are also prone to getting into painful dating situations because of their desire to be matched up with anyone who will pay them some attention. With their uncanny ability to convince themselves that the reason their phone is not ringing is because he lost their phone number or that his drinking at 4:00 P.M. on a daily basis is a nonissue, desperate sisters will dip every nasty habit in confectioners' sugar and swallow it down with a smile. The reason: they "see the good" in him and think they can teach him to be a better person or to love them. The truth is that the joke is on them.

There is a reason "a great match" rhymes with "a great catch." Compromising and understanding that no one is perfect is one thing, but running around picking up reptiles just to have someone in your life is like buying faux Gucci just to have the symbol. Why not invest your money in the real thing and know that it's not going to fall apart at a moment's notice? Don't you dare spend another night out staring at your cell phone hoping "he'll" call! He would have if he were your prince, so move on already.

Raising the bar and setting boundaries is the only way you are ever going to find someone who is worthy of you. Oh, and take your sweet time and do it right. People live until they are one hundred these days, and remember, Madonna found her soul mate at forty-two!

Number Two: The Dramatic Sister

She's so fair, so fun, and so damn loud! A dramatic sister fashions herself a diva (which she mistakenly perceives as a good thing) and loves to put on a show. She thinks of herself as exciting and interesting, but to the rest of us the mere thought of going out with her is like bathing with a hair dryer. Everything—from where to go to the wrenching details of her latest romantic drama—is such a huge production that everyone around her feels drained by the second hour. The ugly truth is she's an energy vampire: she just sucks.

If You Are Acting Out

You love to gossip, are just a wee bit overemotional, and tend to cry when you get tipsy. When a suitor decides he no longer wishes to court you, you pop up at his palace looking to "talk" or deliberately show up at locales you know he frequents. While there, you will stare at him, talk to the people in his court, and eventually put on a performance that rivals Bette Davis in her heyday.

Oh, and did I mention how much you *love* your cell phone? You use it to whine, to call for backup, and to drunk dial lads who have asked you several times not to call. Your Pussycat Dolls ring tone is set on loud, and once you answer, everyone gets to hear you complain about the tragedies you have suffered at the hands of your latest dating disaster. Everyone knows everything about your relationship (or whatever your situation might be) because nothing is sacred. Just writing about you makes me want a bottle of Valium.

Why Changing Will Work in the Long Run

Your emotions are often raw and concentrated, which makes it difficult for a suitor (or anyone else for that matter) to believe in the sincerity of your words and actions. After all, how can anyone take you seriously when everything rates a ten on the scale of intensity? Whether it's professing your love in record time, demanding exclusivity on the third date, or freaking out on him when a female friend gives his cellie a jingle, you usually speed down lovers' lane only to have your potential relationship crash and burn into oblivion.

Acting like this gets you a royal all right—a royal disaster! Suitors may find your dynamic and impulsive behavior exciting at first, but soon, they feel worn out and misunderstood. The truth is no one wants to live on a roller coaster twenty-four–seven!

You are an SRK (serial relationship killer), murdering your reputation and credibility faster than Paris Hilton with a camcorder. The big mess of sex, arguments, and tears that usually comes with dating you makes a suitor feel as though he's trapped in a soap opera that will usually have him running for the exit by date number four. Toning down the explosions, taming the emotions, and turning that damn phone on vibrate will highlight your other, more endearing qualities and calm his fears that you might wind up cooking a rabbit on his stove.

Number Three: The Jaded Sister

With more baggage than Eva Perón on her Rainbow Tour, discussions start out light and airy but soon take a turn for the morbid when the topic of relationships comes up. Still pissed over her ex, who was a total cad and did not deserve her, she often unwittingly makes comments about suitors that make everyone feel as though they are wearing a wool sweater in a downpour. Oh, and please don't bother sharing news about your new prince! She doesn't believe they exist; we know this because she has told us all a million times. We're all sorry she was hurt, but this sister needs to get a grip and realize that the one who did it isn't here.

Do You Leave a Bitter Taste?

Think all lads are lying, cheating, manipulative toads put on this Earth to crack your glass slipper? Yup, a wee bit jaded. Don't trust anyone who doesn't wear a corset? It's time to loosen your strings. As hard as it might be to accept, you're going to have to deal with the issues and stop cross-examining your dinner dates, or you'll be eating alone forever. New suitors are trying to court you because they see and appreciate things in you that your loser ex didn't. Don't behead them for his crimes!

Why Changing Will Work in the Long Run

Are you truly happy existing alone in a locked tower? You better be because it will be just you and your vibrator forever unless you cut down the barbed wire and learn to trust again. It might be hard, but—take it from someone who knows—it's totally doable. Seek therapy, talk to friends, or just take it slow, but remember that you did not do anything wrong, so you should stop punishing yourself. Besides, happiness is the best revenge for the bastard.

Here is an ancient beauty tip: negativity makes *everyone* look dull and pasty. No matter how elegant your gown, if you are jaded, your skin is an ugly shade of angry and your breath is hot and bitter. Now, don't go beating yourself up. It clearly was not your fault that you were hurt. Any maiden who claims not to have had her heart broken is either lying like Cinderella or taking a potion she needs to share with the rest of us. That said, you are accountable for your actions, and you make the decision as to whether or not to be a victim.

In the end the only person who loses here is you. Dating is like learning to ride a bike. You are going to have to face your fears, fall down, and scuff the hell out of your heart a dozen times just to feel the bliss that comes the moment you go speeding down that hill without crashing. You are going to meet some terrible fates along the way, but they all lead up to the one where you find your own happiness. Making blanket statements about "all men" based on the dozen you've known is as unfair as making them based on religion, race, or economics. You are not so closed-minded, so stop coming across as if you are!

Number Four: Sister Self-Importance

This sister can't quite figure out why she's not famous yet. She's a total star! She is fantastic, interesting, and drop-dead gorgeous. Just ask her! She's always wanted to give one of those celebrity interviews she loves reading, which is why she treats every new suitor like an *US Weekly* journalist! From the moment the date begins, the lad next to her stays mute, nodding his head and making his eyes go from wide to wider. He can't get a word in edgewise because she just keeps yapping.

To him, she is just a big mouth flapping away, and he hears nothing but the "Twilight Zone" theme. When he does finally get it out that he loves Mexico, she quickly brings it back to her by telling him about her recent trip to Belize. By the end of the night, he's got enough info on her to snatch her identity, and she knows his name—well, his first one at least!

How to Identify Your Inner Narcissist

You are the most fabulous, interesting, smart, and hilarious maiden in all the land, which is why even *you* love to hear all about you! When your salad arrives, you tell him how excited you are that he already knows half of your life story—and you can't wait to tell him the rest! You are sure he is charmed by your stories about work, your passions, and your friends. I mean, how could he not be? You are so special!

Why Changing Will Work in the Long Run

We all know you have lived one heck of a life, but give him a little time to find out about it. My goodness, woman, where is the mystery? Talking about yourself makes you look arrogant at worst, self-centered at best. Imagine being on a date with someone who brought a book to dinner and just read it page after page. Well, that is what you sound like.

I am not going to pretend there is no fun to be found in talking about yourself, but the most successful people are those who can listen as well. Oprah, Bill Clinton, and Rudy Giuliani would not be where they are had they spent their lives yapping on and on about their favorite way to cut their potatoes. The next time you are on a date with a potential prince, ask him three questions for every one statement you make about yourself. In addition, always ask him something about himself after he asks you something about yourself. This will make you sound interested, humble, and intriguing—which we all know you really are anyway!

Number Five: The Saucy Sister

This sexy maiden loves to flaunt her, uh, *appeal* any chance she gets. With her tightly bound corsets, double entendres, heaping bosom, and six-inch stilettos, she oozes sex, dresses sex, talks sex—and then she wonders why all she gets is sex? Look, being saucy is great, but no one can take two big ones in an extra-small T-shirt home to Mom. Know what I'm saying?

How to Identify Your Inner Vixen

If the hair is colored a shade not found in nature, you often buy your tops in the children's department, or you own a pair of clear platforms, chances are you need to go more Michelle Pfeiffer and less Mariah Carey. Here are some rules: the only thing that looks good in patent leather is shoes for girls ages twelve and below. "Smokey eyes" make you look strung out in the daylight. It's cleavage or leg, never both, and neither before 6:00 P.M. Oh, and one more thing: please, go easy on the self-tanner. You don't want to look like a sweet potato.

Why Changing Will Work in the Long Run

What's hot in the boudoir is suspect on the street. Don't blame me, blame society. You'll definitely get some action, and the toads will love to have you on their arm—but only when their wives and girlfriends are out of town.

Despite what you might have been told by those secretive multimillion-dollar panty company ads, sex appeal comes from within. Indelicate behavior will bring you harsh reactions. As saucy Sophia Loren told us, "Sex appeal is 50 percent what you've got and 50 percent what people think you've got." Right now, you're coming across 100 percent tramp. No one is saying not to show a little thigh, but is there really a need to sex up the Easter parade? Dressing provocatively has a place and a time, and doing it out of that time zone makes you look insecure and outright trashy. The truth is a little mystery is sexier than a full-frontal demonstration. Besides, how cold are you in that?!

Number Six: The Martyr Sister

Sigh! Move over for Sister Joan of Arc. This is the kind of girl who's been through hell and back—and that's just while she's at work. She's always suffering at the hands of evil bosses, witchy-bitchy friends, and slimy toads. If only everyone in the world were as kind as she is, things would be so much nicer, wouldn't they? Well, unless she is sniffing fairy dust, she'll eventually figure out that they aren't and toughen up!

Signs You Might Need to Get Off the Cross

Your friends are never there for you, your fairy godmother abandoned you, and you have to stay late at work because somehow you volunteered to do expenses for your coworker *again*. You never say no to anyone because you want everyone like you, which is why you try to be "nice" but always feel taken advantage of afterward. Your pathetic little monologue starts off interesting but winds up boring suitors to tears, and your friends can't take another long-winded sob story. We've all known descendents of Queen Nasty, and our parents are weird, too, but unless you want to be crying alone forever, you're going to have to learn to stand on your own two feet or no prince will ever slip a slipper onto one.

Why Changing Will Work in the Long Run

A sister who plays the part of the victim in the production of life will never get the lead opposite a prince. Everyone's got pressure and disappointments in life. It's how you deal with the stress that shows character. Is there any chance that, by making people feel sorry for you, you ensure you will always have some kind of attention? After all, who can reject someone they pity? Alas, at some point, every maiden must learn how to tend to her business and live her life as even the strongest prince will tire of being someone's crutch. A prince is looking for a princess, which is an equal. You are just that. Now, prove it.

Here in the real world we treat others how we want them to treat us. So if you're walking around like a pathetic little doormat, you are a prime target for some heavy foot wiping. Taking care of yourself and valuing your time and needs will not only increase your own sense of self-worth but will also change how others respond to you. You must accept that there is absolutely nothing wrong with saying no or standing up for yourself, and in doing so, others will respect you, your time, and your opinion. More laughs, more self-esteem, and better relationships all around—now that's a lovely trade, isn't it?

Number Seven: The Sister with No Self-Esteem

She looks into the same mirror and sees nothing but an accumulation of her many perceived flaws. A night out on the town is devastating to this maiden because every other gal is taller, thinner, younger, and more appealing in her eyes. Dating becomes a bit exhausting because every new suitor is a new identity for her to adopt or another bad date, which further proves her theory that she's not interesting or desirable enough to attract a prince. Everywhere she goes in the land seems to offer up yet another reminder of what's missing in her life.

On the rare occasion that she actually finds herself in a relationship, she usually whips it into a heavy vortex of fear, worry, and lack of trust. She has a big welcome mat on her forehead on which she allows many of the toads she dates to wipe their feet before crossing all of her faded boundaries.

Do You Need to Sew Up Your Self-Esteem?

If you find yourself looking for an underlying meaning in simple comments or have an anxiety attack every time a suitor wants to spend a night out with his friends, there is a good chance you might have a rip in your self-worth. When another maiden shares her good news, do you immediately take her success as a ruler by which you should measure your failures? Do you have a hard time speaking up about things that are important to you? If the answer is yes, it's time to dust the ashes off of that ego and put a little more pride into what you show the world on a daily basis: yourself.

Why Changing Will Work in the Long Run

Low self-esteem is more than a relationship killer. It's so draining that it literally paralyzes your life on almost every level. Not only will suitors grow tired of constantly having to edit their lives and thoughts to keep you from feeling low, but having to convince you of all of the wonderful things they see in you will exhaust them and make them second-guess their initial good impression. Whether it's seeking professional help (which is commendable and nothing to be ashamed of) or making small changes in the way you talk to and about yourself, the only way you will fall in love in the world of dating is to take the time and fall in love with you.

A little bit of confidence can lift you up and carry you around the world like a magic rug. Pull out some of those self-worth oils and dab them on that soiled self of yours before your esteem fades into oblivion. In reality, there is nothing sexier than a maiden who recognizes her value as a human being enough to maintain boundaries and nourish her spirit. What happens if you don't feel it? Then baby, it's time to go faux; fake it until you do! You must never forget that you are your own PR agent, and how you feel about yourself is translated to others in a thousand different ways.

What message are you sending out to the masses? Do you highlight your best traits or point out the ones that make you feel uncomfortable? Are you honest about what you are feeling, or do you go along with a suitor just to have a lad's attention? If you do not care about the one person who has been there for you through it all, the person who has gotten you to where you are right at this moment (yourself!), then a prince is going to wonder how in the heck you can ever love and cherish him (and his future children). Knowing who you are and setting boundaries is also a great toad repellant as low self-image is painted on your face like a bull's-eye.

Number Eight: Sister Superficiality

In these modern times, magazines and television shows exploit the idea that a maiden's hair color or a lad's stock portfolio is more important than her or his value system. Thus it can be difficult to remember that underneath that shell lies a *soul*—with feelings, needs, wants, hopes, and dreams—but remember one must. Whether her basis for placing an overwhelming amount of credibility on the external is based on total oblivion or a lack of empathy, a maiden who does so comes across as vapid and boring. Here is a rule that shall stand the test of time: the only people who wade in shallow waters are toads.

How to Identify if Your Values Are Only Skin Deep

If your idea of a "perfect match" is "tall with blue eyes and dark hair" but you couldn't care less about his desire to have children or his hobbies, there is a good chance you're focusing too much on the packaging. If you know in your heart you would dump your dream guy if he were to go bald, it's time you took a dive into deeper waters.

Why Changing Will Work in the Long Run

If you care more about trivial things—such as how many abs are popping out under his shirt or if he's balding—than how he met his best friend and what he wants out of life, you are coming across as an immature, inconsistent, and unreliable person. What suitor can count on a maiden who will jump ship at the first sign of aging or sickness?

Good looks will wither away, but incompatibility is everlasting. A relationship needs to be built on a foundation of trust and mutual respect in order to last. One based on beauty and materialism is the equivalent of building a house made of sand. The moment there is a storm it crumbles. Even the playboy prince knows this, which is why he might take you out here and there, but he would never invest his heart or future in someone so flighty.

Number Nine: The Sister Who Is Really Queen of Control

This is the sister who wants to control her prince. She has knickers twisted up so tight they cause her to speak in high octaves (which explains all of the shrieking). With a constitution of demands, desires, and agendas, men are often left feeling as though their testicles are locked in a tower just months after they start dating her. She doesn't really like him hanging out with his friends (such bad influences!), and his style needed that update, didn't it? It's hard to see her as his princess when he's so terrified of her.

Do You Need to Ease Up?

You truly believe that your way is the best way to get things done. If he doesn't like it, fine, he just won't get sex/kindness/a night without you nagging. You make him watch "American Idol" when he's dying for ESPN. He must go shopping with you instead of playing poker with the guys. Oh, and while you're snipping at him in the kitchen to cut the cheese cubes properly, his mates are in the living room wondering what you did with their real friend.

Why Changing Will Work in the Long Run

Do you ever hear a faint yelp at night? Chances are that sexy, wonderful prince you started dating is somewhere locked inside of that unhappy lad you've changed him into. That's only if he stayed that long. We all hated being told what to do as children, and it isn't any different in adulthood. The fact is everyone wants to find the person who likes them for what they have to offer, especially a prince. Don't buy white slippers and paint them black with polish, because the real color will always come through, and it will just irritate you and make you look tacky, tacky, tacky.

It can't be comfortable walking around with a rod up your rear, so how's about taking it down a few notches. How great would it feel to live spontaneously and be a little more carefree every once in a while? Why not let the dishes sit in the sink while you ride a couple of rented Vespas with someone special. Life is not a lovely soufflé. It's a delicious, messy, decadent cherries jubilee, so get a little on your starched shirt once in a while and you might find yourself asking for two forks to enjoy it!

Number Ten: The Sister All About Him

She just loves her prince. She adores him, lives for him, and would do anything for him—whether it's making his dinner, dropping off his laundry, or ditching her friends (again) to order in Chinese and watch his favorite movie. This is the sister who stops answering her phone so as not to interrupt their time together (which is never ending) and keeps her phone on high at her best friend's birthday party (because he might call). He is the apple of her eye, but that could be poison.

Is Your Heart Beating Too Loud?

If you find yourself baking his favorite cookies every week or he has enough "sweet little notes" to fill several shoeboxes, there is a solid chance you are in lovey-dovey overdrive, which will crash any chance you have of maintaining an equal relationship. Everyone loves a little sugar as a treat now and then, but just as sugar tastes good, it's also what rots our favorite things.

Why Changing Will Work in the Long Run

Sure, everyone likes a nice maiden, but human nature is to walk on a doormat. We appreciate the things that are uncommon—

dinner at a nice restaurant, a gift on our birthday, a glass of champagne to celebrate good news. However, if you are making every morning feel like Christmas, chances are he's now living on autopilot.

I once dated a man who was spoiled by me. I ran his errands, cooked his dinner, did his laundry, and basically dipped everything in chocolate before handing it over. Then, one evening, to my surprise, Mister Fabulous sipped too much Scotch and confessed to me, "You know, you are like decadent chocolate cake, but no one wants to eat that every single day for breakfast, lunch, and dinner. It's just not that interesting anymore." Whoa. Talk about a wake-up call.

Being kind and docile has its perks, but no one is like that twenty-four–seven, not even sweet little you. Chances are there is something else going on, whether it is insecurity, fear, or even passive aggression. Finding out why you are afraid to show your rainbow of colors and are forcing yourself to jump through hoops will help you to relax and help him to appreciate the little things you do—as opposed to just expecting you to do them, or worse, not even noticing! This does not even take into account the fact that your neglected friendships might start to blossom in the sunshine of your reignited interest in things other than your royal.

Number Eleven: The Sister with the Golden Shovel

She's gorgeous and manicured and loves the finer things in life—as long as they are on someone else's tab, of course. This sister never offers to pay for her own dinner, movie, diamonds, or whatever the night entails. She wants to be spoiled and will take an interest in any suitor who's willing to go the extra mile down Fifth Avenue. Sometimes she'll tell herself that she is "old-fashioned," but we all know that this is crystal-dipped BS, of course.

How to Identify Your Miner

You'd like to believe that you are allergic to inexpensive champagne, and the thought of ever wearing faux anything is enough to send you to the powder room in tears. You hang out at expensive hotel bars and love to bond over bonds. A man's stock rising is more important than his need for Viagra, and a flash of the AmEx Black Card is the ultimate turn-on.

Why Changing Will Work in the Long Run

While a suitor might have the means to grant your every wish and then some, no one likes to feel he is being used or taken advantage of. Those toads who *are* willing to wine and dine you but who won't call you for weeks at a time are well aware that they are buying your time. Think about that. Besides, there is a word for maidens who allow themselves to participate in situations such as this one, and it isn't "princess."

Security is a beautiful thing, but your desire to be taken care of at the expense of love is a sign of major insecurity, and that's just an ugly mole you need to cut off now. When you have the confidence to know that you can take care of yourself, you can be more selective in the person you date. You can enjoy the romance and passion inspired by chemistry and butterflies in your tummy, and not just where he's taking you to fill it.

Number Twelve: The High-Maintenance Sister

This sister loves to be spoiled, relishes bubble baths, adores pink, and refuses to drink beer or sit in any place that serves it for that matter. She has specific needs for everything from temperature and diet to face-washing rituals and bag/outfit coordination. She abhors sporting events or anything that gets her even slightly dirty. She would never eat a hot dog from a street vendor, and the trait she is most proud of is her ability to cry on cue to get what she wants.

Is Your Tiara Showing?

While you might not admit it, you secretly believe being called "high maintenance" is a good thing. After all, high maintenance is the trait that ensures your nails are always perfectly manicured and you are never late getting your waxing. If you are always sending food back, pout when your beau wants to sit and watch a game, or can't go anywhere without your Chihuahua/Louis Vuitton bag/sidekick, chances are you need to stop drowning everyone in your prissiness and learn to go with the flow!

Why Changing Will Work in the Long Run

While a prince is looking for a princess, he does not want one who acts like a royal pain in the butt! It's great that you want to look your best and you know what you like and dislike, but your actions are sending the message that you think you are better than everyone else and have an inability to relax. Sure, men enjoy a woman who looks good, but not at the expense of their enjoyment of life.

Your routine and limitations are taking the fun out of life—not just for you but for anyone dating you! Do you really need to get a blowout three hours before a flight? Would it kill you to meet his friends for a night at the pub as opposed to sitting pretty in the VIP section of some swanky bar? Compromising every once in a while shows a suitor that his feelings matter and that his enjoyment is more important to you than chipping a nail.

Royal Revelations About the Sisters No Prince Wants to Date

"Women should stop taking so many things personally. I understand that women are, generally, more emotional than men, but it becomes very frustrating when something is said or done that is in no way meant to be mean and the female takes it to heart. We then have to spend/waste an hour trying to talk ourselves out of it. Most guys don't play dating games and will be forward about any problem they have. I do believe that most of the reason why this happens is I think women read into men's actions a lot more than vice versa."

—JIM, TWENTY-EIGHT, MANHATTAN BEACH, CA

"I look for a woman who respects and appreciates me. I want a sexy woman with minimal baggage—willing to love and be loved. That's good girlfriend material."

—STEVE, TWENTY-SEVEN, NEW YORK, NY

"Drama is the quickest way for a woman to get herself booted out the door. Nobody wants to date a pain in the ass."

—MIKE, TWENTY-SIX, CLEVELAND, OH

"A woman will ruin her chances with me if she is overtly preoccupied with material things. Asking things like, 'Lawyers make a lot of money, right?' and 'How many payments do you have left on your Lexus?' is a big turnoff."

—ASHTON, FORTY, ST. PAUL, MN

"When a woman claims she is high maintenance, what she is really saying is, 'I am proud of being a totally selfish witch.'"

—MARC, THIRTY-THREE, LOS ANGELES, CA

Chapter 2

Throw Out the Proverbial Bridal Binder!

S o, you wanna get hitched, huh? You are interested in getting a ring for more than just your new cell phone, and like many single maidens, you have zero issues with flipping through bridal magazines just for fun. Join the club, lady! For most of us there is absolutely nothing wrong with popping into Harry Winston (just to look) before he's popped the question. After all, how will we know that a seven-and-a-half-carat flawless cushion cut really complements our eyes unless we see it ourselves?

Well ladies, I have some good news and some not-so-good news. The good news is that you are not alone when it comes to your matrimonial fixation—not by a long shot. There seems to have been a resurgence of gals who are obsessed with getting hitched. We are told that we can have it all: a fantastic career, a loving family, and a great social life. This belief has made us want it all and want it now. The bad news is that marriage-obsessed chicks are not exactly at the top of a lad's list of maidens he is dying to date.

So, what's with the obsession? Where did it originate? Well, this topic could fill up a book in and of itself, but we'll touch upon a couple of the central issues.

Cinderella promised all of us (a) that we would find a prince, (b) that we would marry the prince, (c) that we would do so in a gala event with every adoring eye on us, and (d) that our ever after would be a happy one. Cindy assured all of us that on our big day we would be pampered and polished and that our blood would become our "something blue." We would immediately transform into a princess, even if just for the day. This promise led us to daydreams about our fancy dress, our special slippers, and, of course, our perfect union.

Now, we might swear up and down we aren't excited by the sparkle of it all and know in our hearts that it's the bond not the bouquet that is important, but let's not kid ourselves. Even the most realistic maiden hopes for a touch of fantasy on her big day. In this day of the glamorization of weddings, brides get the royal treatment, but sitting and waiting for your big day to arrive can be a royal pain in the bum.

The Possibility of "Happily Ever After"

With all of this razzle-dazzle to look forward to, it's no wonder we're so damn obsessed—especially when the only thing most of us have to look forward to in our daily lives is our mid-afternoon latte or ordering in from our favorite Thai restaurant while watching reruns of "Everybody Loves Raymond." What makes this a complicated situation is that the Cinderella-style wedding is not impossible to achieve—for some. She didn't lie about the possibility of such a spectacular event, just that every maiden in the land would have a chance to experience it.

Celebrities and royals spend millions of dollars ensuring themselves a day of romance that reaches fairy-tale proportions. Some go so far as to have their big day sponsored (yes, you read that right) to live up to that of Cinderella's. This obsession is great news for florists and caterers but bad news for the rest of us who will have to mortgage our homes and sell our livers to experience the kinds of weddings we read about in fairy tales and tabloid magazines.

OK, so we might not be able to afford a Vera Wang . . . fine. Once we have accepted that, we have to move on to deconstructing Cinderella's most damaging lie—the one that convinced us all that somehow, the wedding and marriage are tied together. She told us that "happily ever after" is a guarantee sealed with a kiss and a band of platinum (gold is so passé). The truth is a day of pretty flowers and happy tears does not guarantee you a lifetime of bliss.

Wait, you don't want to hear this? Of course you don't! No one does! We don't want to be bothered with heavy statistics and stories from jaded divorcées. Not us! We want romance, passion, and thrills! Why think about the future when we can focus on the fairy tale and daydream about our big day, right? The idealism of our wedding day and becoming legally bound to a handsome lad is pure magic, and it's been working a spell on us gals since we married off our first Barbie doll to that handsome Ken. Unfortunately, Mattel didn't provide a reality check with the plastic bouquet (must be in the same place as Ken's genitals).

Why do you think it is that getting married was introduced to most of us as a goal, not an option? Why is it that our dolls had veils and our binders had the names of the boys we liked scribbled all over them? The answer is kind of a sad one. For centuries, maidens have been passing down Cinderella's tale as fact, though none of them have experienced the magic and bliss she promised all of us. Notice that our suitors don't play "house" or marry off their transformers. Think about it: how many lads do you know who walked around with our names paired up with theirs on their folders and book covers?

For most of us, there is a very special place in our psyche reserved for the day we are asked to marry someone and another for our big day of "I do's." We plan our lifetime of happily ever after, and it all starts with a simple trot (or dash!) to the altar. As I stated, this obsession is not your fault. It's Cindy's. She swore that getting hitched would bring us a whole new life— one that far exceeds the one that we could have ever obtained while single. Cinderella conveyed the message that getting to our happy ending would be effortless. Hell, she got it all with just a few wishes and one hot night of heavy flirting. In fact, if we are to believe Cindy, if you act like her you can get your beau to pop the question in fewer than forty-eight hours. Remember, she's a liar.

It's time to find out how to deal with meddling family members who are determined to marry us off (and make us feel like crap for not doing it sooner) and learn what we can do about our own altar anxieties. We'll also discuss what is going to happen if we don't get some control over them. It's high time that we address some of the truths Cinderella omitted from her story.

Slow Down! You're Not in a Race to the Altar

It's time we get down to brass tacks or, in this particular case, platinum bands. Whether they are swimming circles around the lads in their dating pool or frantically gasping for air as they doggy paddle from date to date, there a whole lot of maidens out there who are kind of freaking out right about now. The reason: they want their future to turn a deeper shade of committed and are turning purple as they sit holding their breath for it.

How many gals do you know that have picked out their wedding colors? Ever hear about a friend's engagement and feel a sickening belly twist right in that area where your happiness for her should be? OK, who are we kidding, ever gone in and actually tried on a dress? As I mentioned earlier, most maidens dream about becoming brides like lads dream of being rock stars and sports heroes. It's not always that we even want the man; we just want that damn dream wedding. They might not admit it, but like our male counterparts think about doing the horizontal tango, many maidens who are creeping up to or past their own personal designated age of "old-maid" status think of a relationship at least a dozen times a day. Still, there is something preventing them from moving forward with their walk down the aisle. They're totally barefoot.

Now, I could tell you getting the slipper is all about timing and your ability to control yourself (and it is), but we both know you don't want to hear this. You want answers, and you want them NOW! So I will give them to you, but you have got to listen closely and change your approach almost entirely. You've got to chill the hell out, settle down, and relax no matter how old you are, how many of your friends are hitched, or how badly you want that destination wedding in Madrid.

Know Yourself, First

Saying "I do" promises nothing more than a piece of paper that confirms you said it. There is a big difference between wanting to share your life with someone and being so obsessed with getting coupled up that you start to despise being alone. That difference is how much you like yourself.

How much value do you place on your life and your achievements? How well do you know yourself? Are you able to be honest with yourself and truly identify your motivations for wanting to be married? This last one is a biggie. I mean, no one is discounting the incentive created by the chance to don a gorgeous gown, but one night as the big star of your own rubber chicken and $6,000-band soiree is not a good enough reason to cry over not being engaged (no matter how hot you'll look in that dress!).

Look for a Prince, Not a Husband

How many times have you heard the advice from older family members or read a book promising the fail-proof way to find a husband in a short period of time? In most cases, the author or advice giver sees getting hitched as the main goal, with a mate being more like a wheel on the side of the overall plan. Unfortunately, this kind of approach to dating is disastrous, and here's why. It's like those guys who order brides from magazines. It's about getting the body and not the person. Approaching finding a partner in the same way you would buying a bookcase is so . . . um, well, it's certainly not romantic, let's just say that much.

Finding and marrying a lad is not the same as picking up your dry cleaning; therefore, it should not be treated like a box on your to-do list. Your goal should not be to "get married" or even to be with someone; it should be to get to know yourself and be happy with who you are and then find someone who will love, respect, appreciate, and cherish you while growing with you as a human being.

The idea that guys are to be snatched up like handbags is pathetic, outdated, and boring. There are plenty of suitors out there, so don't rush around playing the mad dating dash and exhausting yourself by thinking every great guy you meet is going to be your prince. Sometimes things are not going to work out and that's OK. That's what makes it so darn special when it does! Just relax and realize that life is not some kind of race. No one has the right to set a timer next to you—even you. This is your life that we are talking about—and as far as we know we have only one—so please, stop waiting to meet someone before you take the time to enjoy it. Take some time to get to know yourself and different suitors and you might just have a blast while picking the person you want to spend the rest of it with.

Until you get to know him, a lad is just one of many suitors who could possibly be carrying your slipper. If he is, he is one of your princes and you can think about marriage as long as he is on the same page. Even if he's a perfect match, a proper courtship takes time. A bond needs to be created before anyone will get anything more. This bond should be unique and based on more than a few itemizations you might have on your perfect-guy wish list. Also, it's important to remember that while society maintains this feeling of implied intimacy, you cannot possibly know someone in just a few weeks. How can you know a person it took twenty-five, thirty-three, or forty years to become in just a few dates over a few weeks?

Let's Get Real: Getting Married Is No Fairy Tale

With celebs marrying after weeklong courtships and friends eloping in Vegas wedding chapels, getting hitched is treated like a novelty pit stop—much like taking a photo at the Eiffel Tower. Look, they're a heck of a lot of fun most of the time, but weddings should not be viewed as just big parties with more focus on the veil than the vows. With the frivolous way society treats these events, it's no wonder that many maidens do not view marriage as the huge undertaking it is. Getting married is the thing to do, and once we hit thirty or thirty-five, we start to squirm with discomfort if we don't have a ring. This need to keep up with the Janes and to commit can leave us acting like we should be committed.

Having a relationship is a beautiful thing but only when you have paid close attention to the person you are planning to commit to. The choosing of a mate is something that should be taken very seriously, and it requires more than just chemistry and good intentions. It requires a significant connection and a true understanding, appreciation, and respect for one another. These are things that cannot be forced or rushed through in a speed-dating event. As I said earlier, you are going to need to toss out the books and beliefs that you can find a husband in thirty days or less. Think about that anyway. How much can you possibly know about someone in such a short amount of time? Do you even know someone after six months or a year? It takes that long to get a review from an employer, and you're thinking of legally binding yourself to someone in less time than it takes to ask for a raise? You're not organizing your finances here. You are looking for someone to spend the rest of your life with. You do the math. When it comes to making a lifelong commitment to someone, there are bigger things to focus on than having a constant date to parties and getting to go on a honeymoon. Do you share the same main goals for the future? Does he share your value system? How do you both handle stress? Are you on the same page when it comes to having children and/or rearing them? Are you a workaholic while he envisions the family eating together every night? What are your ways of handling money and spending? These are things you need to ask yourself and each other.

As much fun as it would be to believe that we all can go from meeting Mr. Wonderful in the grocery aisle to taking a walk down one in no time, unless you are on a reality show, this is not going to happen to you—and, if it does, say no. Also, please do not take the previous statement as a suggestion to try and find love on a reality show. I have produced these things. Trust me on this one.

The Ring Will Not Change Your Life

Cindy told us that marriage and contentment go hand in hand. Thanks to our idealism, many maidens will happily buy into this lie despite discouraging divorce statistics and a high percentage of failed relationships. We chicks want to fall in love and believe that, when we do, our lives will become everything we dream them to be. Suddenly we'll be happy all of the time and our jobs will become tolerable. Our bad habits will fade away and a bright, positive light will seep into the nooks and crevasses that were once filled with doubt and negativity. Worse, Cindy has many of us believing that love should be easy and effortless and that marriage is the ultimate culmination of love that will whitewash our lives. The reality is that we are totally kidding ourselves.

By now, we should know that nothing in this life is guaranteed, and certainly most things worth having are not just given to us. Now, the positive side of this is that we have quite a bit of power over how our lives turn out in that we can choose to work on all of the things that make us unhappy, so that when we do meet the person we want to spend the rest of our life with, we won't bring these things into the relationship and bog it down.

The fact is, marriage might provide a sense of security in a relationship, but it will not change what lies at the core of each

individual (and remember that you remain individuals even if
you share a name, home, and electric bill). If you hate your job
and have issues with your self-image now, you will be the same
way once you get married—only you will bind a poor prince to
your issues. If you are dating a demanding, arrogant bastard,
don't fool yourself into believing marriage will change him into
a kind, understanding partner. The only thing that will change
is that you'll wake up legally linked to a demanding, arrogant
bastard the day after. Cinderella's flawed promise has many of
us believing the world somehow changes just because we got
two signatures on a marriage license, but before you go bliss-
fully running to the altar, remind yourself that you are the only
person able to change your life, and it will take work.

Nor Will the Ring Change the Basic Fundamentals of Your Current Relationship

Remind yourself that if you are dating someone seriously and
you marry him, you will have the same kind of relationship
you had before you got married in the sense that he as a human
being will still have the same moral fiber, the same idiosyn-
crasies, and the same annoying habits. In fact, his traits might
magnify as years pass! He will still be the same lad he is right
now, only it will cost a lot of money to leave him. We often
assume that getting married will allow us full access to some
kind of fantasyland where we will be happier and more content
with our lives. This will not be the case unless we are happy and
content with ourselves. It takes two happy and healthy people
to create a happy and healthy relationship, no matter what their
marital status is.

Another sad truth is that relationships that feel magical at
one point might not be that way years later as circumstances
change. You both will continue your inner development as indi-

viduals. This means that your boundaries might change, your goals might become incompatible, or you might find yourself falling out of love with your partner. This is hardly romantic, but it's real. If this is a possibility that every couple faces, imagine Cinderella's reality. This gal married someone she barely knew! If you do this, you are sure to find quite a few surprises in the many days to follow, and they probably won't be that he likes to bring you milk and cookies before bedtime. Lust at first sight fades, and when it does, look out because personality and pet peeves can be monster dragons to slay.

So what is the lesson to learn here? Getting married is not the goal; making a commitment to a partner who makes you happy is. Saying "I do" is not going to make you any less anxious, mend broken promises, or fix a mismatched pair. In fact, walking away from a bad match and an incompatible relationship is a whole lot harder and more expensive when you've uttered those vows.

R.F.E.D (Ring Finger Erectile Dysfunction) Does Not Have to Ruin Your Life!

Much like the penis has been known to control the minds of the lads of the world, the minds of single maidens are often taken over by a body part that loves to distract us at the strangest moments: our ring finger. At weddings, it maliciously taunts us during slow dances, and on blind dates it immodestly exposes its naked flesh. At bars it has been known to make us drink too much and cry in small bathroom stalls. Then there are the dreaded family gatherings where it can make us say terrible things to our grandmothers when they ask why it's not dressed for the occasion (more on that later). Every time a handsome stranger walks by, it pops up and leaves us with a terrible case of the blues at whatever ball we are attending.

Oh, and can it ever make us lie! We'll say and do just about anything to release the pressure, but unfortunately, getting the opposite sex to comply with our "carnal" desires for a ring can be difficult. The painful truth is that living with R.F.E.D. can be both frustrating and humiliating for everyone involved, especially you. What's worse is that curing it takes more than becoming exclusive.

In fact, the side effects can actually worsen once you've slipped the slipper on. One maiden recently admitted to breaking down in tears when she opened her e-mail and received the engagement announcement of a friend who had been dating her boyfriend for a year. When this maiden's suitor walked into her castle, he found her in a fit of tears and asked her what was wrong. She explained and, WHAM, she immediately began down the path of pressure that inevitably had a negative effect on her relationship. Pressure uses force, and force—even subtle force—is not natural. She'd have fared better by watching him move at his own pace. This way she could have observed his actions and have had a better understanding of who he was and whether he was right for her.

So you see, the obsession with finding that damn finger a ring to slip on affects most maidens and can snowball into something extreme. Thoughts about relationships and marriage can become an addiction, and when this happens we have to treat it as such.

Take a Moment and Figure Out Why You Want to Get Married

Wanting a companion is normal. Focusing on your unfulfilled dreams of "happily ever after" as the bride of Prince Wonderful to the point of tears is unhealthy and destructive. Sit down and really think about why you want to be married, why you are in such a rush, and why you are allowing yourself to be depressed over something you cannot control.

Dumb diamond delusion aside, I am hoping that you, by now, have taken the *Bridal Dreams* subscription off of the renewal cycle (or at least thought about it) and that you have stopped wasting your lunch break surfing the new wedding gown collections on various designer sites. If you haven't, do it now, lady (and use that money to go see your favorite matinee idol with friends).

It's time to sit back and ask yourself a very important question. What are your real motivations here? Why is it that you really want to get married? Don't convince yourself you are excited about a joint checking account if it's really all about the honeymoon. Another thing: don't allow your age to dictate how you should feel about your single status. Being thirty-five is not a valid reason to want a ring, I'm sorry. These are two very separate aspects of your life, and besides, you are not as old as you think. To an eighty-year-old, forty is still a young, hot mama.

Now, I am not saying it makes you a bad person to fantasize about your wedding day, but to allow it to have a choke hold on your current happiness is unfair to the woman you have earned the right to be at this moment. Looking forward to that white dress and veil is something that is practically badgered into our heads since birth. Being a bride is actually an option for Halloween! But how many little grooms do you see out there? And of course, there are our mothers, who talk about the day we marry as though it will be some kind of out-of-body experience. I blame all of this on Cinderella, who claimed she found the passageway into a flawless existence by uttering a simple "I do."

That said, none of these are valid reasons to beat yourself up for not having the option of a hyphenated name. If you are trying to keep up with your engaged friends or trying to appease your mother, you need to admit this to yourself and realize that your life is your own and your journey is unique and you don't have to follow anyone else's rules or tire yourself out trying to keep them happy or live up to their expectations. They have their own life to live and should focus on theirs and leave you to make yours anything you want it to be—on your own time. Take out a pen and paper and write down all of the reasons you want to be married. Be honest and jot down everything that comes to mind (don't worry, you can burn it later).

Let's Discuss Your Answers

Great! Did you figure it out? Were you completely honest? I am putting my trust in you!

Now let's discuss what you have come up with. Once you have answered why you want to be married, ask yourself what that has to do with sharing your life with the right person. If the reasons are closely connected, write down how taking your time is proving beneficial. Are you learning more about yourself? Moving up in your career? Traveling and gaining a more worldly view? I have found this exercise is a fantastic way of releasing some of that anxiety that has started to hoard in the corners of your psyche. It's like a psychic massage.

Wanting the feeling of companionship is a perfectly normal desire, and, hell, if you want to spend a few nights hosting your own little whine and cheese soiree, be my guest. However, if you are punishing yourself for not having found what you think you will find with a certain someone—and you are talking down to or about yourself for being single—we have a problem. Are you spending your precious days yearning for something you don't have or convincing yourself that you have passed an age in which you could have or should have found it? If so, you are partaking in small rituals that are diminishing the enjoyment of your life. This can not only have a negative effect on your mood but also affect the way you treat and come across to others—both of which will most definitely have an effect on your dating life. Who wants to date "the desperate sister" or a miserable maiden?

Here in the real world, self-bashing implies that you do not respect yourself and that you find your own life and time alone unfulfilling. This behavior suggests that, like Cinderella, you are waiting for someone to swoop in and provide you with the exciting and balanced life that you think can come only with a coupled or married you. No lad wants that kind of pressure.

Think about what your actions are telling the world. You are saying that even you don't find time with yourself fulfilling and fun. How do you think you are selling time with yourself to the masses of lads out there who are available to date you?

Because of Cinderella's lie, we have formed a terrible habit of projecting our happiness right into our daydreams of an ideal relationship or partner, all the while ignoring the many reasons we have to be happy at the present moment.

We sit around wasting our days as we count the ones until we are matched up. We miss out on the joy of appreciating our many accomplishments and blessings because we are so focused on what we have not gotten to on our life's time line. Happiness is always about the future and never in the present.

When we meet someone, we'll be happy. When that person and you are exclusive, it will be better. Once in a relationship, it becomes about the next step. It then becomes, "When we are engaged, it will be amazing." "When we are married, we will all spend our days in spotless houses, taking picnics and falling madly in love over and over again." In these scenarios, happy endings are a free gift that always comes with someone else, and it remains one step ahead of us. Like the donkey and the carrot, we are making an ass out of ourselves while we follow the carats.

This becomes a vicious cycle that can leave the most optimistic maiden feeling blue.

Here's the truth: happiness is for individual sale, and unless you buy into that, then the only guy you are going to find and keep is a toad in the discount bin. No one wants to date someone who needs another person to stay comfortable in their own skin or who is constantly looking toward the next step in order to be happy. That's a lot of pressure and faith in something that may or may not happen. Codependent behavior by maidens is not only condoned in modern society, it's nearly encouraged. The fact is, being married to someone isn't love; being in love with someone is love. This pressure we put on ourselves and others is a major issue, and issues get in the way of healthy relationships.

Undoing the Curse

I am so proud of you! You are making some serious progress here! Owning up to the fact that you are a wee bit preoccupied with the big day allows you to identify the root of the problem for what it is. An obsession is defined by Dictionary.com as a "Compulsive preoccupation with a fixed idea or an unwanted feeling or emotion, often accompanied by symptoms of anxiety."

Clearly, this is not how any single maiden should be spending her days. It's downright exhausting! Take a few deep breaths, and remind yourself that you are wasting your time stressing over something that is a nonissue (the urge to beat yourself up for not being married, rush a relationship to the chapel, or allow yourself to worry about something that has not happened yet). We do not have the aid of a fairy granting wishes here, but that does not mean you need to feel helpless or have to allow your situation to shatter your dreams. It just means you have to work the circumstances of your life to your advantage. Reality is not a bad place to live, and it is painful only when we resist it. But once we accept it, we will find that it can be a powerful ally.

Let's take it on, shall we? The fact is that you are not engaged. You may not even be dating. This doesn't mean that you are destined to die alone; rather, as of right now, you will not need to worry about wedding dresses, cakes, or registering. You need to relax and use this energy to improve your life and self-worth and to go out and meet someone with whom you might fall in love and eventually marry.

This is not meant to depress you by showing you how many steps away you are from the big day. However, it should shake enough sense into you that it forces you to realize you are literally wasting time being miserable. Every moment you spend loathing life or complaining is gone forever. You are literally losing moments of your life being miserable! Instead, you could be utilizing all of that energy and putting it into something that is going to benefit your life, such as working out, going out, or joining a new club. Fill up those moments and make them meaningful to you! Perhaps you could take all of those dream-wedding ideas and throw yourself a fantabulous singles party where you have every friend bring one single male and female acquaintance outside of your circle.

Voilà! You'll meet new singles, and you get to bake monogram cupcakes and dress up without winding up in tears.

Your Relatives Do Not Have a Right to Point the Finger

They all mean well, right? After all, it really does matter to your newly married cousin Penelope that you get hitched. It has a direct impact on the enjoyment of her life. Sigh. Then, of course, there's Mother, who has been daydreaming about your wedding since you came into this world with a big "ta-da!" You love her, but if she calls you one more time to ask if the gent you just met is coming to Thanksgiving dinner, you'll scream, especially because it's March.

With all of their unsolicited advice, small interrogations, and concentrated assessments of what you do wrong, it can be hard not to allow their comments and actions to chip away at your self-worth. Alas, we've got to create some boundaries here. As much as we love our family and friends, we have to make it clear that we have our own lives to live and they have theirs. Now, no one is saying to knock Aunt Myra on her caboose when she asks if you have been seeing someone. But you can politely let her know that you are enjoying your life and that you would appreciate it if she would ask you about your new spinning class or your trip to Spain instead of who you met there.

Many maidens grew up believing Cinderella's lie and cannot comprehend that we can possibly have as much fun walking barefoot in the sand as they can donning a slipper (more on that in Chapter 4). You can do one of two things to get a handle on this situation: you can start keeping your private life your own little secret until things have progressed into a phase where you have significant reason to believe it's not just a fling, or you can simply feel free to remind them every time they step on your toes. As an adult, you have the right to protect your feelings, and speaking up does not make you a bad person. Remember that.

Be Realistic About Your Past and Present Situations

Is there anything worse than being so sad upon hearing about your friend's engagement that you actually start to miss a toad? Suddenly your ex who made you cry every other week wasn't so bad, and that lad with the anger issues was "really funny." Look, hindsight may be twenty-twenty, but it's hard to see clearly when you are wearing your rose-hued specs. When we are looking back on failed relationships or ones that never fully blossomed, we all can fall victim to airbrushing over the ugly parts and polishing up situations in our minds. It's easy to see the unrealistic in past and future images, but these are mirages in a desert of loneliness and fear and must be treated as such. This is counterproductive in terms of actually focusing on meeting a solid match. In addition, convincing yourself that you missed out on something fantastic will only make you feel terrible because you will start to believe you lost something better than it was and, worse, that something better will not come around again.

You're kidding yourself, and you are doing it because you are fearful and anxious about not being in a relationship. Remember, there is power in identifying what is at the core of your emotions. First, if it were so fantastic, it would have lasted. Even if you are the one who screwed it up by crossing his boundaries, sending the wrong message, or not putting your most authentic self forward, it wasn't a good situation because you were not good for him. Therefore, it was not a good match. This goes both ways; lads deserve loving and respectful relationships as well. Remind yourself that you have a significant amount of quality matches out there, lady. There is no such thing as "the One," only "one of"s, but more on that later.

Either way, whether it was due to a mismatched pairing or bad timing, there was a reason things didn't work out. You can learn from those reasons and move forward, accepting new opportunities with a newfound understanding of what you want and what you are able to offer your partner.

Pay Attention! There Are Opportunities Popping Up Constantly!

OK, back away from the phone. Throw out Angry Andy's number already, and, for the love of yourself, delete that text you were about to send to Cheating Charlie! Why are you going to waste your precious moments playing emotional ping-pong with a fixer-upper when there are literally dozens of single suitors out there ready to meet you? If getting married is important to you, it can happen, but only after you have made some changes and put your best self on the market. Only then will you find a solid match because you will have worked out your own kinks. Do you really want to attract a perfect match for a desperate/sad/anxious gal? I thought not.

There is a prince for you to marry out in the land, but you are not going to find him unless you change your attitude and outlook, tame the obsession, and pay attention to the world around you. Clearly, the way you have been living isn't getting you the results you want, right? Just like you need to change your eating and exercise habits if you want to lose weight, you'll need to go on a dating diet if you want to trim the excess fat in your romantic life.

It's so funny that we sit around wondering where all of the good guys are, convincing ourselves and each other that there's some kind of royal shortage in the world when they surround us every single day. Think I have snorted too much fairy dust? Pay attention. Who do you think surround you in the coffee shops, the gyms, the local wine tastings, and bookstores? Do you live on an all-female island? Just as you run your errands, go to work, play, and live in this world, so do millions of available men. The issue a lot of us have is that we get so caught up in our own thoughts and preconceptions that we don't take the time to open our eyes in both the literal and theoretical sense. An amazing thing happens when you make the decision to take on a new approach to life; you become aware and alive. Your reality starts to change even if the world remains the same. We need to remember that we are all living through our own experiences, and while we can share them with one another, no one's view of the world is going to be exactly like anyone else's. Perception is an amazing thing. Our thoughts, feelings, past experiences, hopes, and desires can warp our view of reality. When you rewire what's inside, you are guaranteed to have a whole new experience outside. That's the point of this book! So, if you are so focused on hosting your "poor-me pity-party" that you simply aren't recognizing your many potential princes smiling at you in the cafeteria, your personal space has a big, fat "Do Not Disturb" sign all over it and potential princes are reading the fine print. Maybe it's time to take it down and replace it with a bright, inviting "welcome" mat! (Just make sure it's not on your forehead!)

Toss Out That Damn Time Line Once and for All

So your name is not hyphenated yet or you are not even in a committed relationship by the big three-oh, four-oh no! or whenever; is it really the end of the world? Do you really feel all that different after the anniversary of your birth? I mean, if you just broke up with humdrum Harry two months before your thirty-ninth birthday, should you be beating yourself up for not being married, or should you be celebrating the fact that you recognized a faulty connection before committing yourself any further?

Setting personal goals is a great way to stay motivated in life, but the surest way to feel terrible about yourself is to give these goals an expiration date. Life does not sour just because you haven't done something on a set schedule; nor does it toss aside the possibility of you reaching these goals later in your life. Always remember that here in the real world there are various personalities, circumstances, and opportunities coming at you daily, which is why it is important that you stay flexible.

If you want to meet someone new, then do or try something new! Sitting around, doing the same old thing, visiting the same old bars, and hoping your prince will come riding in on his white horse is a fool's game. The right goal is to want to meet a respectful, loving partner, not to have him by age twenty-six. Accept your life as it unfolds, embrace that it is unique, and acknowledge your creation of a lot of what is happening in it. There is a good possibility you have been married to your career or babying your friendships. Every life is different, and creating a time line for your life is a dangerous habit. Break it before you let it break you again. Carrying your expectations around like an old ball and chain is only going to slow you down.

Perfect Only Comes in Chocolate

No matter what Cinderella said about her guy, perfection does not exist in human beings. Nor does it exist in romantic situations. What is excellent in theory usually winds up flawed in application because people are unique and utterly imperfect.

The problem with Cinderella's wedding lie is that it has not only raised our standards to an unattainable level but has brainwashed us into believing that for some maidens, it is actually possible to attain. This belief has resulted in a society that believes in the BGD (bigger, grander deal) and the FTR (fairy-tale relationship), which has resulted in some serious emotional brain damage and shattered hearts.

This desire for some kind of deity in the form of a lover has us ignoring and turning away wonderful suitors simply because they don't measure up to this ridiculous ideal. We concoct relationships in our heads that do not allow for the interruptions caused by the twists and turns of life. Waiting for a "perfect match" is as silly as waiting for the moon to sing. It's never going to happen. Besides, there is something to be said for passion and arguments. Ever heard of makeup sex?

Life Is Not a Romantic Comedy, and No One Should Be Acting

Whether it's confusing love with the unrealistic situations we see in the movies or comparing every guy we meet to the fantasy we project on some matinee idol or crush, sticking your hopes into an image blinds you to a plethora of solid royals. It also depresses you. It's very easy for a maiden to get so caught up in her fantasies that they ruin her ability to see the real world clearly. She's raising that bar so high that the Almighty would have a hard time getting a second date!

The worst part of this is that, even when in a good and solid relationship, we tend to criticize our partners or dismiss the connection because they or the relationship are not causing us to screech with excitement every day of the week. No one will bring you flowers every day or even once a month forever. It just doesn't work that way. Each individual has his or her own unique traits and interests, and everybody gets annoying sometimes. Enjoy romantic comedies with your suitor, but don't expect to live one.

Get Off of the Misery-Go-Round!

How many times have you told yourself there is no one out there who is decent, only to stay in alone? Ever been the one to avoid going out with friends because you don't want to "bear the disappointment" of not meeting someone new? How about going out and pouting because you have not met anyone, as your friend chats with a new suitor close by? If these scenarios sound familiar, don't beat yourself up. You are certainly not alone.

Dating can be hard when you are tossing your hopes and dreams into a bar every night. It's time to collect your dreams and put them away for safekeeping while we address why many of us subconsciously look for ways to rationalize our beliefs that there is no one out there. We do this as a way to soothe our own egos. We want to prove that the reason we are not connecting with anyone isn't because we have some kind of issue; rather it's because the good guys are taken or emotionally broken. It may not be true, but it works, right? Acting like this might cool the burn for a short period of time, but it's never going to heat up your romantic life. Motion creates motion, and if this is your attitude, it's stiff and dull.

You Do Not Have a Fairy Godmother (Sorry!)

As lovely as it might be to sit and count on hope, faith, or a great matchmaker to make your dreams of love come true, the reality is that there is no wand to tap your life and make it all you hope for it to be overnight. You, and only you, are solely responsible for creating your own magic. The great news is that this leaves you in control to wash away the dark outlook that is clouding your judgment and commit yourself to taking a positive and proactive stance as opposed to a negative and reactive one.

Don't forget, I too grew up with great expectations about relationships and believed that fate or some other magical force would provide me with a happy ending as long as I was a good girl. Needless to say, I remained single (and in terrible relationships) for a long time. Then I took the time to reevaluate what it was that I wanted in a mate and what I was willing to change and do to open myself to the possibilities of finding the decent partner I was hoping for.

I wrote down everything I was feeling and was in for quite a shock. There were expectations coming out of me that no lad could meet. It was then I knew I was building a wall based on a fairy tale, and it was separating me from dozens of fantastic suitors (and possibly my prince) until I broke it down.

You Can Rewrite Your Tale Any Time You Want To

Now it's your turn to confront your massive wall and tear it down. Take out a piece of paper and write down everything you are looking for in your prince. Don't be afraid to write down the craziest hopes and dreams. If you want a man who looks like a young Pacino and carries diamonds in his pockets, say so. Just be HONEST!

Once you have written these hopes down, take some time and really evaluate them. Ask yourself if these traits are realistic and if you can find these qualities within yourself. Once you stop limiting yourself to "tall, dark, handsome, wealthy, fit, perfect, from Maine," you can start paying attention to all of the lads who surround you and find one who makes you happy, shares your love of wine, and can introduce you to his hobbies. Better yet, you will have the peace of mind that comes with putting a halt to the subconscious habit of trying to prove to yourself that because your ideal does not exist, it is not you who has issues to resolve but an entire gender! What a relief it is to know that you have the ability to change your outlook and therefore change your romantic life. Besides, who says you have to have a full head of hair to be intelligent, warm, and sexy? Stop limiting yourself!

Calling all authors!

Now, grab that proverbial pen again (the one with the cute pink feather), and get to scribbling because you now have the important task of writing your very own fairy tale; you know, the one where you run barefoot in the sand, enjoy your life, and save yourself! It may sound like a bit of a cliché, but every single day is nothing but a blank sheet of paper—a twenty-four-hour block that offers a fresh opportunity to change the pace, tone, and direction of your life. You decide what your lead character will think, feel, and do. Will she be proactive or reactive? Will she give up or move on? Will she embrace life and take risks or be trapped in her routine? Every page you write will lead up to your ending. The question is: Will you make sure it is a happy one? Will your story be interesting, or will it be the same thing on every page? Will it be a comedy or a drama?

If you wind up writing a tragic tale, take note: most of the time, disappointment comes when we have stopped thinking, thrown our expectations on autopilot, and found comfort in feeling miserable. Our bad habits create a bad situation, which creates a bad story and a terrible ending. Think about it? How many Valentine's Days have you started to mope over in January? Now, don't be ashamed. There isn't one of us who hasn't eaten the whole box of chocolates while putting curses on those who didn't have to buy their own from the local drugstore. But the only thing whining and moping will bring is extra pounds in the middle and a bunch of memories of holidays wasted feeling sorry for yourself.

We ladies have got to realize that, despite what we tell ourselves (and each other), being single right now doesn't mean we're serving a lifelong sentence. Every big event we attend without a "plus one" is not a failure in our emotional review. Sitting in misery over being single is like sitting in *a* cell with the keys in your lap. You have the power to change your outlook, and by doing so, you will change everything else in your life. It's the romantic butterfly effect. Remember, living your life with only you to think about is a grand opportunity to really get to know who you are, take that great Italian class, or enjoy time with your friends. Most important, it keeps you unattached to toads and attending balls, which is where you are going to meet your prince.

Reality Check

Marriage-Minded or Wedding-Obsessed?

When you think of the reasons you want to get married, what do they include?
A. I am hoping to find a solid partner first and then to create a family and share our lives together.
B. A Vera Wang gown, pink tulips, and a Tiffany registry.
C. I am not getting any younger!

When you think of your ring, what do you think about?

A. The person who loves you enough to give you a token of his affection, who cares about what it looks like; it's what it means that counts.

B. Cut, color, carats, and clarity—all set in platinum, thank you!

C. Give me one from a gumball machine; just sign the damn papers.

When your friend announces her engagement, what do you do?

A. Congratulate her on her exciting news. You know she'll do the same when you meet the right guy.

B. Let her know where you think she should register.

C. Burst into tears and grab a bottle of cheap red wine on your way home to your cat.

You are thirty-five years old and unmarried; how do you feel?

A. A little disappointed but glad you held out instead of settling.

B. Bummed; your dream sheath dress is so outdated now!

C. Devastated; you're pretty sure you will never meet anyone at this age. It's all over.

Your newly married best friend comes to you in tears. She thinks she made a mistake tying the knot. What do you do?

A. Tell her it's perfectly normal to be a little nervous after the big day, but remind her that her happiness is what is ultimately important so, if it isn't the right guy, there are more out there.

B. Tell her how sorry you are, but explain that she will need to consider the fact that cream gowns don't come in as many options as white ones do.

C. Get angry with her. How inconsiderate to complain after getting what you want so badly!

What are you looking for in a mate?

A. Someone who shares your passions and has a good heart, a strong value system, and a hearty sense of humor.

B. Someone with a big enough trust fund to afford your dream wedding and your monthlong honeymoon in Belize.

C. Someone with a pulse and a few strong sperm.

Your mom takes another swipe at your single status at dinner. What do you do?

A. Remind her that you have had a lot of dates but want a love affair as romantic as hers and your dad's was.

B. You aren't paying attention; you're surfing Martha Stewart Weddings online for tips.

C. Say nothing; she's right—you are an old maid.

How did you do?

Mostly As: Good for you; you're a healthy, marriage-minded maiden. With a focus on the meaning of the day and the partner with whom you will share it, you don't place unnecessary pressure on yourself or your relationships, instead opting to go with the flow of your romantic life and hold out for the best possible match. Think you are a sensible single? I do.

Mostly Bs: There is no denying it; you love weddings—the dress, the diamond, the flowers—but what about the marriage? Getting hitched is more than an evening in a white gown with a gorgeous veil; it's a lifelong commitment to another person. Until you find that special someone who becomes a bigger incentive than your bridesmaid dresses, it's best to keep your d-cut diamond a treasured daydream.

Mostly Cs: Weddings make you cry, but not for the right reasons. With a boatload of silly expectations and missed deadlines, you're in a constant state of self-doubt. Marriage is the merging of two lives into one, and the more you convince yourself you need to take what you can get, the less likely you are to merge with someone who will suit your lifestyle or even meet someone because you are sending out the sign that you are desperate and miserable. Take a step back, relax, and remember, this isn't a competition; there is no race to getting down the aisle to the altar!

Chapter 3

---·◆·---

Don't Shove Your Feet into Slippers That Don't Fit

*A*CCORDING TO CINDY, a slipper was a shoe. But what have we learned? Cindy fibs a lot, which means we need to take her words with a bit of salt, right? The truth is a slipper is a whole lot more than just a shiny stiletto that gives you a little height and forgives a little excess in the caboose (which if you didn't know, it does). It is actually the term used to describe the culmination of all of the traits a suitor is looking for in his mate. Some of these traits have to do with beauty and style, but unless this lad is a total toad, he's looking for a whole lot more in the maiden to whom he gives his shoe than her bust size and eye color.

Lads are just like us in that every single suitor you meet has a core value system, moral character, and ideals. He has likes, dislikes, passions, and dreams about his future and a basic understanding of what he is looking for in a mate. Just like you, he has a group of family members and friends that he is hoping you will get along with and quirks he hopes you can learn to love. If he also desires a family, he wants to know that you are the one to bear, influence, and help to raise his children.

Know What You Want Before You Go Shoe Shopping

These core beliefs and desires are what we call his "slipper," and every suitor is carrying one. The question comes when he allows you to try it on—will it slide on effortlessly, meshing well with your lifestyle, hopes, and values (aka your foot)? Or will it make you scream out in agony after walking the first block? Will he like the way it looks on your tootsy, or will he want to take it away a few moments after allowing you to try it on?

If it is the former, there is a good chance you have found one of your princes. I say "one of" because there are hundreds of them out there who would all mesh beautifully with you. But if it is the latter, you've got to walk on.

No matter how much you want that shiny stiletto, like the design, or value the attention it brings, if the shoe doesn't fit, you've got to put it back atop the shelf. By trying to wear it, you are taking on the agonizing and utterly exhausting task of trying to shove your lifestyle, hopes, dreams, and personality into a place they cannot flourish comfortably. You're also selfishly scooping up someone else's prince and leaving yours at the ball forcing everyone to settle. Do you really want all of that on your conscience? I didn't think so.

Besides, going for the mediocre fit is hardly giving yourself the best options, lady. You might be one of those maidens who truly believes that having a slipper is better than going barefoot (if so, please read Chapter 4). But the reality is that when it comes to picking the person with whom you are going to share your life—even if it's for a month—you owe it to yourself to be selective. By placing a high value on your commitment and to whom you give it, you are better equipped for the ball known as "the world of dating." There is absolutely nothing negative about knowing what you want or who you are, and it's downright admirable to be honest about it (this includes being up front with yourself). In fact, taking time out to evaluate these things allows you to worry less about getting a damn shoe on that foot and more about finding something you can walk in *and someone you can walk with* and still be comfortable.

What is really more important in the long term? Having the instant gratification of a slipper and committing yourself to a relationship in which you will be less comfortable in the long term? Or walking barefoot and holding out for a perfect shoe—one that fits properly?

Chances are if you choose the instant-gratification approach, the relationship or your mental state is going to end up cracking anyway, as bad relationships have a tendency to bring out the very worst in us. The bottom line: no matter how much you want it, you've got to be patient and choose quality footwear over a blasé pair and painful bargain. You simply have to adopt the motto of the dating-savvy maiden: if the slipper doesn't fit, keep shopping.

Most Slippers Are Not Going to Fit You (but Don't Worry, Many Will)

If every suitor is carrying only one pair of slippers in one particular size, you don't have to be a math genius to understand that the odds of your fitting into the pair carried by every lad on your dance card are low. It is for this reason maidens should not allow themselves to give so much credit to the ones that don't fit. Expecting that every suitor will want you to try on his slipper and that it will fit (or that you will want to wear it even if it does) is setting yourself up to be knocked over every time things don't work out, and being knocked over is no fun. So, he's nice and you're lonely; that's a perfectly normal situation, and it happens a lot. For goodness sakes, please don't go pretending you feel a connection that is not there! That is just a painful disaster waiting to happen.

The key to avoiding a lot of heartache in all aspects of your life is to accept every situation for what it is and not try and make it something else. Moving on is a whole lot easier without having to lug around unnecessary baggage. Also, by living here in the real world and seeing things for what they are, you maintain control over your self-esteem instead of placing it in the hands of people you barely know, which often leads to adopted insecurities. In the short term, his slipper might look great on your foot. However, as any maiden who has ever struggled through an evening wearing the wrong size knows, there is nothing more painful than a fit that's too tight or more annoying than a too-big slipper falling off every five minutes. This doesn't even take into consideration the fact that wearing the wrong shoe for days on end is one hell of a way to blister your personality. At one point, the discomfort will become your only focus. It's quite difficult to be wonderful, patient, kind, dateable you when you are feeling constant pain or frustration and trying to fill in empty spaces with random materials just to avoid going barefoot.

Keep this in mind when you're out at the ball. While you might be attracted to a certain suitor, his sarcasm might become draining over time. You might like to lead while a strapping fellow keeps expecting you to follow. You may enjoy a sexy suitor's conversation but find the way he tortures your toes with his flawed quickstep terribly disappointing. The idea is to try on as many slippers as possible to find the one you are happy with, the one you are comfortable walking in, and the one that fits your wardrobe and lifestyle. Until then, it's perfectly OK to walk barefoot. Hell, it's even great when you do it in the park on a warm summer day.

The Size Might Be Right, but the Timing May Not Be

There is a great saying I heard from a young lad back in high school. "Time means nothing, but timing is everything." I didn't get it back then, but after doing the dating tango for many years, I understand it completely and could not agree more. So do many of the men I have interviewed.

Think back to that wonderful guy you dated—the amazing lad with the charming laugh and the ability to send you into a tizzy with a bat of his long lashes. Remember how much fun you had dating him? You got along fabulously and you just knew he was your prince, when out of nowhere, he stopped calling and said that he was not ready for a relationship with a maiden like you. It was not you, it was him, he explained. He was just not "in the right place." He swore on his manhood that this wasn't an easy letdown. He seemed totally sincere, but of course, you didn't believe him. How could you?

Dating books and relationship experts have all explained to you that a lad who likes you is always ready to commit and will do anything to be with you. According to them, a suitor is ready to commit, and if he doesn't, he just doesn't want to commit to you. So, instead of taking his words at face value, you did what every other maiden would do in your situation. You decided to overthink it all and torture yourself. Instead of going out with friends and meeting someone new, you stayed in night after night trying to figure out what you did wrong.

First you thought it was your hair. Then something you might have said. Finally, after weeks of self-examination and too many phone calls with friends, you realized you hadn't acted like a sister no prince wants to date (Chapter 1) or vomited your emotional issues all over him (Chapter 8). No, you had been lovely—a total catch if you say so yourself. So, after realizing how fabulous you were, you jumped out of the pity pond and ran far across the land to the other extreme where you simply wrote him off as a toad, a total uncommittable jackass who used you. That is, until you saw him six months later with his new fiancée.

His Aha! Moment

So what in the hell made Mr. I-Am-Not-Ready so ready that he bought a ring?

Well, it's simple (but not any less painful for you, sorry). Your guy had his "aha!" moment. You see, somewhere in between the time frame in which he stopped dating you and the moment he popped the question to Miss Has-Nothing-Better-to-Offer-than-You-Do, your suitor had an "aha!" moment and was anointed an *emotionally available prince (EAP)*. But, unfortunately, this all came about after he freaked out and tossed you off of his horse.

It sucks, but it happens to the best of us, and we've got to realize that sometimes it really isn't anything we did or did not do. While it's true that a suitor will commit to the right maiden when he sees her, this can happen only when his eyes are no longer glazed over with idealism about bachelorhood. Only then is he able to recognize a good woman when she comes along. This clear vision is possible only after he has had an internal discussion with himself and decided that he does in fact want a partner and that he's financially, mentally, and emotionally ready to share his life with someone exclusively.

This decision is never an immediate one. It takes a lot of time for a suitor to decide to hand over his commitment. It's important for us gals to remember that our suitors are not like us. They're not from another planet, but they are wired a bit differently. We can try and deny this all we want, but after interviewing thousands of men and women, it's clear: we just don't think the same way when it comes to romance, friendships, or much anything else.

Men are a lot simpler than we are when it comes to their thought process and application of that process. They are not less intelligent, mind you, just less emotionally attached than we are to fairy-tale promises, hypothetical situations, and even current experiences. The reason is that most of them weren't lied to as we have been. They don't place the value of their lives on whether or not they are with someone, married, or in love, and they don't base their hopes and dreams on the women they date. We could learn a lot from our male counterparts in this department. They own their life and make us a part of it. We often don't acknowledge ours until we make them a part of it.

For them, a relationship is one of many priorities, but rarely will they beat themselves up for not having one. If their families are nagging them to get hitched, they let it roll off of their backs. His mother calling him a "confirmed bachelor" is taken a lot less hard than your mother reminding you that you are a bridesmaid yet again. They also have the added benefit of society and family members not constantly encouraging them to settle or bend their boundaries "just to have someone."

Even if they have met someone, men have to have achieved other goals before making a relationship with that someone a top priority. In spite of what Cinderella shared with us about her prince, in the real world, most guys are not romantic Don Juans who are worried about rescuing us on a white horse. Sorry.

As you know, we are much different. In our world, romance is the theme of our life's movie. It's often our ultimate goal (and if it isn't, it certainly shares the top spot with whatever else we are into). It doesn't matter if we are twenty-two or seventy-two because most of us are happy to commit when a great guy comes along (sometimes he doesn't even have to be great, just male). Our suitors are a bit different. It takes a lot more than love and connection to get them to hand over the slipper and finally the crown. While most of us are ready to fall in love at any age, our suitors are less apt to idealize the idea of settling down with one maiden for the rest of their lives.

He Has to Actually *Want* to Give Away His Slipper

While magazine articles and dating books might promise you surefire ways to manipulate suitors and romantic situations to get him to commit, the reality is that free will is a bitch and no lad is ever going to settle down unless he wants to. There is absolutely nothing any maiden can say or do to convince a suitor who wants to remain a bachelor to give up his wild ways and trot off into the sunset with her.

A good question is why would she want to? If a gal has to run down a list of her amazing attributes, he clearly doesn't see them and is not worth her time. The bottom line is that it doesn't matter how fabulous or stable you are or how gorgeous you look in La Perla, you're not going to get your foot into that shoe until he decides he wants you to wear it.

He Has to Be a Randy Royal for a While (and So Do You!)

You may be the best thing he is ever going to find, but he won't realize it until he has sown those oats. And don't kid yourself either, ladies, this is not an outdated figure of speech. There are oats to be sown. I am hoping you already know this because you have had some fun yourself (and if you haven't, get out there!). Even Cindy's "perfect" guy went to every maiden in the land to try before he settled down with her and gave her slipper back to her. I happen to think it's an excuse that the ol' guy used to get one last hoorah, but hey, that's just me.

Now, I am not suggesting that you should start sleeping around (you shouldn't if you are looking for something more than sex), but the basic fact of life is that sex is a lot of fun, it feels good, and lads have a knack for experiencing it without shame or emotional attachments. I am not saying I agree with it, but the fact is that our suitors have no issue with enjoying many maidens before they settle down with one. Now, not every guy needs a few dozen notches on his post, but most agree that everyone, male and female, should break a few loaves of bread, dance a few dances, and toast a few cocktails with a variety of partners. A suitor simply needs to date a variety of women before he will ever figure out that you are filet mignon among low-grade beef. No matter how many of his friends adore you or how many times your friends remind him of how great you are, he's going to have ants in his pants until he's danced around with a variety of ladies at the ball. Try and rope him in before he's had his fun, and you're setting yourself up for a miserable prince who feels he missed out on something. Ignore your own dating desires, and you'll wind up feeling the same thing.

He Wants to Know That He Has the Best Maiden He Is Going to Find

While Cinderella lied to all of us, airbrush technicians and Hugh Hefner have been telling tall tales to our suitors. They are the reason our guys are holding out for a Jessica Alba look-alike who can cook like their mothers, make them laugh like Dave

Chappelle, clean like their maids, and keep silent while they watch World Cup replays.

The search for the bigger, grander deal is common throughout the land, and it can bite relationships right in the romance department. It's the reason they want a Victoria's Secret model and we sit in relationships wondering why our guy isn't all of the great things we project onto Matthew McConaughey or George Clooney.

This all sounds like a bunch of superficial crapola, but it really isn't. Our suitors value their single status, and they hold on tightly to it until they feel they have found someone worthy of tossing it aside. We can learn a valuable lesson from them in this respect. Your commitment is something worth holding onto until you have found someone you really enjoy being with. Don't just give it to the first person willing to take it! Our male counterparts may be kidding themselves in thinking any of us will meet the unrealistic expectations brought on by *FHM* or Vickie's ads, but we have some crazy ideas of our own when it comes to relationships! The point is that most men don't want a girlfriend for the sake of just having someone. They want the best person they can get. Let's adopt that mantra, shall we?

He Has to Want to Share His Life, Heart, and Personal Space

Have you ever sat with a suitor you liked only to have him completely zone out? How about having a lad tell you he wants to stay in and be alone rather than meet you out at a new hot spot? Our male counterparts need a lot of downtime (called "cave time" by one suitor). This is something most of us do not understand and will take personally because it is in our nature to communicate feelings, share our space and time, and bond over socializing. Most lads out there are not as inherently communicative or nurturing as we are, and while we might want to "be there" for them, they see time spent with us as less relaxing when they have something on their minds.

This can make having a serious relationship more difficult for them. The idea of having someone involved in most every part of their lives, having to consider someone else's feelings and needs, and having to talk things out when all they really want to do is sit and play video games is just daunting to them. The reality is that no matter how much a lad likes you, most guys look forward to watching the game alone in their flannels without worrying about how you will feel about it. Guys enjoy solitude and relish doing their own thing more than we do, which is why no matter how much he likes you, unless he has made the decision to give up some of his free time, he isn't going to commit. As I said, our suitors place a greater value on their personal time than we do. To them, being single is something that offers a slew of rewards that we tend to ignore.

He's Got to Know He Can Afford You

Now no one is suggesting you are a gold digger, but for most suitors career status and a solid economic foundation are things that need to be considered before settling down. The fact that he lives at home with his mom or is broke may not mean much to you, but it's no laughing matter to him. In fact, placement in the economic totem pole is of major importance to most of our male counterparts. For them, career and social status are embedded in their desires much like relationships and marriage are in ours.

Many of the men I interviewed have told me they would like a girlfriend "but cannot afford one." The reality is that most suitors are not born into royalty like Cindy's guy, but they do share his chivalrous desire for the ability to provide something of significance in the relationship. Most suitors want to feel that they can stand on their own two feet and possibly even take care of you, if need be. This is true of even the most egalitarian lad. Unless your guy is a toad, no suitor worth your time wants to feel as though he's living off you or not carrying his weight financially.

If your potential prince feels as though he is not where he needs to be in his career or financially, chances are he won't be focused on having you by his side—no matter how fabulous you are. As for his career, men are bad at multitasking; they compartmentalize. This means even the most romantic prince has an ability to stop the pitter-patter of his heart in order to focus on getting his career in order.

What This All Means for You

Even if you are dating a guy who enjoys your company and meshes with you on many levels, unless he feels settled—that he has experienced his life and will not be hindered by committing—and has exhausted his romantic resources, then there is a good chance you might be competing with his fantasies and idealistic visions of what lies in his future. This does not make him a toad any more than your fantasy issues make you one, but until these issues have been resolved in his mind, you will never get much more than a few kisses and a spin around the floor.

What this all means is that you truly might be the amazing maiden, you might have made sure you are not a sister no prince wants to date, and you may be drop-dead gorgeous inside and out, but that won't matter to a prince who still wants to spend his weekends playing rugby with the boys. So, instead of blaming yourself, battering yourself emotionally, or taking on his issues and trying to convince him of your greatness both as a person and as a couple, it's best to take the slipper off and walk yourself over to a suitor who's ready to meet and date you—now.

Reality Check

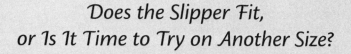

Does the Slipper Fit, or Is It Time to Try on Another Size?

When movie night rolls around:
A. You both love Woody Allen flicks, Vietnamese food, and Diet Sunkist.
B. He'll endure a romantic comedy if you'll watch the latest cheesy vampire flick.
C. You don't like the same kind of flicks, so you just avoid movie night altogether.
D. He makes you go to the movie alone while he sees *Basic Instinct 2* with his friends.

When it comes to vacationing:
A. You love Mexico, he loves Spain—you both love to travel.
B. You can't get enough of the ocean, and he's all about camping and hiking.

C. You want to see the world, but his idea of travel is to visit Atlantic City.

D. He loves to travel, just not with you.

His mother:

A. Hugs you hello.

B. Says to say hello to you when she calls.

C. Doesn't really approve of your background, and he's not about to "make waves."

D. Referred to you as "one of his girls" to your face.

The last time you were sick:

A. He showed up with flowers, soup, and your favorite DVD.

B. He called to see how you were feeling.

C. He told you he'd love to be there but he had a friend in town. Besides, you wouldn't want to get him sick, too, would you? He didn't think so.

D. Yeah, he doesn't "do" sick.

Friends:

A. His friends have become one big group with your friends.

B. His friends all know who you are, and he attends your friends' parties with you.

C. His friends love yachting in Nantucket, and yours love pizza and bowling down the street.

D. His friends have met you several times but never remember your name.

When it comes to the future:

A. You share the same basic dreams: marriage, children, and a house by the beach.

B. He wants to move to SF, you love NY, but the core value systems match up.

C. He would never leave Perkiomenville, but your dreams are to be realized in London.

D. He doesn't talk about the future unless it's later that night.

His sense of humor:

A. Rivals Vince Vaughn's; he's hilarious, and you love it!

B. He's no stand-up comic, but he's a hell of a guy and you love him!

C. You don't really know when to laugh; you don't really get him.

D. Is sarcastic and offensive.

Physical attraction:

A. Is a nonissue; he's the sexiest thing even with his soft tummy!

B. He's no model, but he makes you so happy you airbrush right over his acne.

C. Theoretically he's gorgeous, but you just don't feel that "thing" for him.

D. His six-pack is smooth and his brows waxed; he's so hot! Just ask him!

When it comes to letting you know how he feels:
A. You know where you stand; he shares his feelings with you constantly.
B. Sometimes you wonder where you are headed, so you ask and he comforts you.
C. He's talking marriage, but you can't focus, because you are thinking about your ex.
D. You're analyzing his every move but know not to ask him; it will scare him away.

How did you do?

Mostly As: Congrats! The slipper fits! Are you sure you didn't create him? You have definitely found one of your princes and are lucky enough to have found someone who really shares your likes and dislikes as well as your value system. He seems to respect you and the relationship as well as share basic desires, wants, and compatibilities. There is something very special about a relationship in which you can be yourselves, communicate, and have fun together. Remember this during the silly little fights that every couple has every now and then.

Mostly Bs: The slipper is a little tight, but you can stretch it out a bit. It's not a perfect fit, but you don't have to keep shopping either. It's perfectly natural to have different ideas, needs, and likes as long as you respect one another's differences and are willing to compromise here and there. Not only is a perfect match nearly impossible to find (unless he's a clone), it can be boring in that it's easy to get caught in a routine. Different likes and dislikes and personality traits keep things fresh and can make for some great and passionate discussions. Learn from one another, and celebrate your differences.

Mostly Cs: Ouch! It's not your size. He's a great guy, but he's not your prince. Heck, he shouldn't even be one of your suitors. Your values are different, and your desires are different enough to cause major conflicts. If you are constantly jumping through hoops to find commonalities or find the relationship more frustrating than fun, it's better to walk barefoot.

Mostly Ds: What slipper? He's a toad! I cannot believe you are wasting your time with someone who devalues you the way this creep does! You are a wonderful girl, and while you might act a little wacky here and there, you certainly do not deserve to be mistreated. Toss this creep back into the pond and keep walking.

Chapter 4

The Joy of Walking Barefoot

HE GREAT THING about the world we live in is that there are dozens of opportunities for gals to enjoy themselves—regardless of whether they are dating, married, or taking time off from men altogether. I know it may sound a little wacky to hear this when we live in a world obsessed with coupling up and maidens are crawling on top of one another to slide their foot into a slipper. Better yet, by taking advantage of various opportunities to get to know themselves and develop new interests, they enhance their character and fill their lives with interesting experiences. Maidens who take some time to walk barefoot open their minds to new ways of living, and yes, they even up their chances of meeting new, interesting suitors who share their passions. It's a win/win situation when you take time to actually live your life instead of just exist in it.

You know, it's funny. As smart as we are, we gals can really come to some dumb conclusions sometimes. One of the dumbest and most self-defeating: making the decision to link the joy and fulfillment of our lives to our romantic status. It's just plain sad how many maidens toss aside the significance of the many achievements and blessings in their lives once they remind themselves they don't yet have a prince. Suddenly, their friends have to remind them of their amazing bonds, great social connections, strong career, solid family ties, creative talents, and other wonderful achievements because they have spiraled into an abyss of sadness focusing on what's "missing" in their lives.

They'll wonder why they can't meet a guy, why he doesn't call, and why everyone else has someone (PS: most people do not, hence this book). What they don't realize is that their life is a gift given to them, which means they can unwrap and wear it any way they want to. They own their life and unless they are comfortable wearing it, like the way it fits, and have tailored it to their liking, they're not going to feel their best no matter who they're dating.

Not knowing who you are is like wearing a wool sweater in a downpour. Besides, no one wants to date someone who places so much pressure or emphasis on being in a relationship . . . but more on that later. This is the maiden who will find that she acts catty and jealous when another gal floats past her with a dreamy new beau, which can be especially disturbing when it is not in her character to act in such a way.

Your Life Has Significance Regardless of Your Romantic Status

So, why does this happen when we know we are strong, emotionally intelligent, and well accomplished? Why do we act nasty and bitter to other coupled-up women when we don't mean to? Well, it's simple. Cinderella told us that snagging a prince was the ultimate prize. Now, this might have been true for Cindy—I mean, she didn't have the same options we do. She wasn't focusing on breaking glass ceilings, getting her master's degree, or getting to her kickboxing class on time. This girl was scrubbing door screens and being bitched at by a mean old woman her father married; she was just dying to get out of that house! She didn't have friends. She couldn't get a job. There were no Pilates classes in Far, Far Away.

Now, you might feel as though you can't curl up with a law degree on a cold winter's night, but does that mean you should be any less fulfilled by it? Of course not! While Cinderella hammers home the idea that marriage is the ultimate happy ending, our reality allows us to enjoy many other rewards. These days finding someone is one of many exciting experiences we have the chance to enjoy. Unlike Cinderella, maidens today have the opportunity to really live out their dreams, and they are smart enough to understand that the real happiness in life is found with fulfillment in all of the areas that they create.

Your relationships with friends, the hard work you put out, and the beautiful gifts of time and kindness you bestow upon others create your foundation as a human being as well as your legacy, and no one can define or create that but you. This means that while companionship is a viable need, it is neither your only need nor is it something that will fill in the gaps of the other areas if they are missing. A man will only enhance and reflect what is already there. Your life is a reflection of what you put out, and there are mirrors all around you. The question to ask is: "Am I happy with what I see?"

So while Cinderella wants us all to believe that marrying a lad is the only way to bliss, you have to understand that unless you are a whole and happy person alone, you will not be able to participate in a whole, happy relationship with a prince. We often forget that we will be us regardless of what our romantic status might be. If we are unhappy, unfulfilled, and insecure, we will bring this into our relationship.

Cinderella Missed Out: Sometimes Being Single Can Be Magical!

Cindy made a big mistake rushing into marriage with the first lad who showed her a little attention. She never had her own place to decorate the way she liked it or enjoyed a night in with a foam green mask and comfy old jammies. She never felt the excitement of a first kiss on numerous occasions, and worse, she never took time to get to know herself.

Being single not only means that you have the opportunity to enjoy ultimate freedom of accepting dances and dates with a variety of suitors, it also means that you have the time to hone your criteria for a mate. You are taking the time to see who is out there and figure out what you want out of life, what you want from a partner, and what your deal breakers are. Knowing what your deal breakers are is essential—as so many of us don't find out what will crush, disappoint, and offend us until we have been crushed, disappointed, and offended. We have the chance to tweak the ugly habits and groom unruly thought processes without anyone being the wiser. Why deem such a blessing a lonely curse, when being single is a ball and each date is a spin around the floor with a potential suitor?

I know you want that slipper, but you must always remember that slippers come in pairs, and two is good only when they match. So, instead of looking at every date as a failure if it consists of nothing more than a nice meal or cocktail, realize that you have learned more about what it is that you want and you've practiced the art of the dance. Just because there wasn't an earth-shattering connection doesn't mean that all men are toads or that all the princes are taken. It simply means that the slipper didn't fit, and the suitor you met wasn't your prince. One maiden's suitor is another maiden's prince, but a toad is a toad. That's why it's important that you hold out for the one you really connect with. Leave the little wart monsters in the dating pool and the suitors on the dance floor where their princesses can find them! If you are spending your precious days obsessing over settling down, you're more likely to settle, which isn't fair to you or your future partner.

Your life is meaningful because it's your life. It belongs to you, so take notice of it and enjoy it! Walk barefoot in the park instead of trying to shove your foot into a slipper that doesn't fit. Take a painting class or horseback-riding lessons. Evolve as an individual, and suitors will take notice, but more important, *you'll* have a more fulfilling life—no proposal required. (But you might find yourself with a sparkle on that finger a little sooner once you make the change.)

Stop Reminding Yourself to Be Miserable!

I know its fun to daydream, but is there a truly valid reason to stop into the jewelry store and look at rings on your way to getting your morning latte? Do you really need to compare yourself to the twenty-six-year-old bride on the cover of *I'm Married and You're Not* magazine? Weren't you having a fabulous day until you popped onto Iain'tgotnoman.com? Many times we allow ourselves to overlook bad habits because we are so used to the routine that we start living on autopilot.

Start to really pay attention to how you feel before and after you participate in your little rituals, and ask yourself what you can use this time to be doing that will make you feel good about yourself. Instead of looking at Martha's new wedding cakes, look up a new word or a review of the hot new restaurant you're dying to try. Pass by that jeweler and pop into that great new card store to grab some invitations for a wine-tasting party for all of your friends. It's a shame how committed we are to making ourselves feel inadequate at work, about our bodies, socially, in the world of dating, etc. The truth is that life is full of possibilities to feel good about yourself; you just have to recognize them.

Let go of the idea that being single is some kind of ailment you need to overcome, and accept that being single is where you are in your life and it's not a bad place. Wanting to connect with someone is normal. Who doesn't enjoy the company of others? But trashing your single status or placing yourself in situations where you know you are going to wind up melancholy and miserable is far crueler than any stepmother I have ever heard of.

How You Can Weave a Little Magic into Your Single Life

It's time to do a little magic and rearrange your mind's eye. You need to take off those blinders, open up those heavy pity curtains, and allow the sunshine to flood the way you view yourself and the life you are living. Pull out the mirror and view yourself in a natural light—free from your dark perceptions and imagined flaws. That nasty single mole you hate? Well, it's actually a beauty mark, so dab a little pencil on it and conceal the self-doubt that's gathered around it.

Take a piece of paper and write down a description of yourself in the third person. Pretend you are trying to set up the hottest, greatest guy you know with you. What would you tell him? Would you go on and on about your funny-looking toes, or would you tell him all about your volunteer work, silky red hair, and bright green eyes?

Living solo may not be a fairy tale, but it can be an exciting, interesting, eye-opening, and powerful experience. It's perfectly normal to want to find someone to share your life with, but spending every day bashing yourself for not having met him is a little masochistic. There are enough people out in the land to make you feel insecure and point out things that are less than pleasant about you and your life; you don't have to be one of them.

Celebrate Your Birthday!

The tale of Cinderella made being single sound like the ultimate punishment. Why else would every maiden in the land don her best threads to rush to the ball in the hopes of getting a lad to notice and marry her? The reality is that Cinderella hated her life and needed someone to attach herself to—pronto.

Because of Cindy's emphasis on snagging a lad, most single gals do not realize that life doesn't begin with a kiss from a prince. This realization begins the day you are born. I am not talking about the day your mother brought you into the world, either. Your birthday is the day you embrace yourself and all you want out of life—the day you decide you're not going to wait for a boyfriend to see Italy or try out that amazing new jazz club downtown. It's the day you decide that your life is to be enjoyed all of the time—and not just the times you share it with a handsome suitor.

Open Yourself Up to New Possibilities

As romantic as it may sound to be with someone, it's a hell of a lot of fun to be on your own if you take the time to actually embrace your freedom. Now I am not about to forgo wanting a partner or to promise you window shopping with friends will ever give you the same kind of butterflies as a saucy kiss (unless you are at Pucci, in which case it might be close), but there are a lot of amazing things you can be doing right this second that beat whining about your solo status. You might even meet your prince doing one of them. After all, what better place to meet a suitor than one that expresses a common interest?

You don't need a fairy godmother to work a little magic in your life; you can do it yourself by opening up your mind. This isn't a single girl pep talk, and I am not trying to convince you that your life is something it's not. This is about real chances at filling your life with more than a bar scene and (gasp!) speed dating. Oh, and you don't have to follow all of the suggestions, just the ones that appeal to you. Clearly, "go white-water rafting" is not a valid suggestion for a single gal living in Manhattan who hates the water. The point is to actually take some time to court yourself. Just because you aren't dating a guy does not mean you're not committed. Every moment you are not dancing with a suitor is an opportunity to date yourself, commit to a cause, and write your own happy ending.

Get Your Tongue Wagging

It sounds so cliché, but why not learn a foreign language? If you really follow through, you will wind up learning more about yourself and another culture than you ever realized possible. Don't just take Italian; learn all you can about the country! Invite classmates over for a potluck with everyone's favorite Italian dishes, and save up so that you can treat yourself to a trip to your favorite region to practice all you have learned (and meet some international suitors along the way).

Interested more in art than the art of language? Check out your local museum. You don't need a date to appreciate beautiful paintings, sketches, and sculptures, and besides, no one will nag you to hurry up in the gift shop. Take the time to appreciate each piece, learn more about the ones you like, and open up a side of yourself you might never have known existed. Education is far sexier than three-inch slippers.

Give Back

There's something very special about someone's decision to give their time and energy to help make someone else's life better. Volunteering your time will allow you to focus on what others are facing and might help you count your blessings.

Whether you're signing up to be a Big Brother or Sister, volunteering at a homeless shelter, or offering free tutorial services at your local high school, you're making a positive difference in someone's life. An added bonus? You'll also meet like-minded folks and expand your social network with empathetic and caring people.

Exercise Your Demons

If the thought of walking on a treadmill leaves you running for the hills, don't sweat it. No one is saying you need to become Annoying Aerobic Annie, but there is something to be said about taking the time to get your heart pumping and work out the stresses of the day. Many maidens don't realize that they internalize their concerns; and whether it manifests itself in tense shoulders or wider thighs, getting active will absolutely change your life. Not only will you become healthier, but you'll feel better, look better, and have more energy. Watch your self-confidence soar as you break your own personal records!

Not really into hitting the gym? Get out there and dance somewhere other than the ball! Call up a local dance center or YMCA and find out about salsa, hip-hop, jazz, or even tap classes. You don't have to be a Fosse fanatic to enjoy getting your groove on, meeting new people, and learning about something different and unique. Besides, you'll burn calories, use muscles you did not know you had, and feel übersexy after sashaying to some salty Latin music.

Be the Hottest Hostess in the Land!

Everyone loves a good time, but many people don't take the initiative to set up happy hours and wine tastings. Why not take charge? I'll bet there are some great hole-in-the-wall restaurants in your city that are sure to tempt your taste buds without breaking your budget. Pop onto Citysearch.com, or check out the Arts & Entertainment section of your local paper and find a few places you'd like to check out. Invite friends for a monthly dinner get-together, or pop in for brunch for a cheaper option.

Wanna save some cash? Host a game night. Have everyone bring a bottle of their favorite wine, make some tasty little appetizers, and host a mean game of UNO, Monopoly, poker, or Balderdash. Friendly competition and good conversation with friends is enough to bring out the best in anyone.

Treat Yourself

Is there anything lovelier than unwinding in a superlux spa with the warm glow of candles and the delicious scent of eucalyptus, citrus, or vanilla wafting through the air? It's like a vacation right there in your hometown. Whether it's an hour-long facial or a three-hour package, taking time to wind down and think of nothing other than how great you feel is rejuvenating—not only for the area being pampered but for your soul as well. It also reminds you that you are worthy of extra special attention and care—a fact many of us tend to overlook.

Or maybe you're dying to make a change but need a nudge. Interested in turning that mousy brown shade into a rich chestnut, bold blonde, or ravishing red? Have you been thinking about trying out a new style? Go for it! Set up a consultation with a colorist at a popular salon, or call your local department store to meet with a personal shopper.

If it's your home that needs a little touching up, start your own little renovation process. It doesn't matter if you live in a castle or a shack, it's what's inside that counts. Your surroundings are a reflection of you and how you feel inside. What does your home say about you? Are you hoarding things from your past? Does your soul need a fresh coat of paint? Is it time to toss that boring old throw and shake things up in the bedroom? Look through a few magazines, pick out some ideas you'd like to duplicate, and then commit yourself to spicing up your relationship with your home. After all, it's where your heart should be.

Grant Yourself a Wish

Always wanted to write a novel? Interested in acting? Got a talent for jewelry making? Why not use your free time to see if you can actually turn these dreams into goals and finally into reality? Make a lunch date with a mentor, find out how to get started, and go for it! You might wind up changing the course of your life. Trust me on this one. I did it, and you're reading the results.

Twenty-Five Things
to Enjoy Before You Commit

1. No ESPN v. VH-1 arguments.
2. You say Chinese for dinner, and you say when.
3. Flirt with as many guys as you'd like, guilt free.
4. You get to enjoy more than one "first kiss" until you find the last one.
5. No fights over the remote, which side of the bed, or that damn toilet seat.
6. Two words: his mother.
7. You don't have to share—it's all yours, whatever it is.
8. Drinks and weekend trips with your girlfriends.
9. You can enjoy your guy friends without having to convince him of your platonic status.
10. You get to spend your money on luxury goods like that hot new handbag instead of obligatory anniversary presents and birthday soirees.
11. No sport support; there will never be a football game on your screen unless you want it there!
12. No waking you up after late nights out with his friends.
13. No bachelor parties in Vegas to suffer through.
14. No "female" friends to irritate you.
15. No compromises about where to spend the holidays (and no having to spend money on him, his parents, his cousins, or his boss).

16. Free entry in the club and free drinks at the bar from the cute bartender who wants to ask you out. (Though, I have to warn you to proceed with caution on that one.)
17. If George Clooney calls, voilà! No baggage.
18. Xbox and Halo will never make you late for dinner or keep you awake at night.
19. Biscuits in bed? No problem!
20. You get to wonder and dream about the future and what it holds, which can be a lot of fun.
21. Eat the whole cake during the 1:00 A.M. Julia-Roberts-a-thon, no judgments.
22. You can join a gym, go hiking, go camping, or go skydiving because there is no one there convincing you to do what they like or telling you they "don't feel like it."
23. You're totally free to be yourself, and the more you're with yourself and being true to who you are, the less likely you will hide that beautiful spirit just to get a lad to like you.
24. One hundred pairs of shoes become 101 pairs of shoes, and the only thing you'll hear is your inner shoe freak screaming "Yippee!"
25. You want a cat, you get a cat.

Chapter 5

Having a Ball in the World of Dating

*S*o, HERE YOU are: a saucy, single maiden who has exorcized her dating demons, has stopped obsessing about the ring, and has instead taken a vow to love and respect herself. You have learned that you don't need a slipper to find love and happiness; you need the right one. You have learned to accept your life for what it is and not what you hope it will be in the future.

Congratulations! You are now officially ready to get out there and start dating again! You'll still be the same wonderful maiden in the same city and town, and you'll be surrounded by the same suitors, but you wouldn't know it. Dating is about to feel like a totally different experience! This time you'll be at the ball donning a brand-new outlook and a sexy understanding of who you are and what you want. Suitors beware!

In order to do this, we are going to do a little refresher course and understand what the laws of courtship are here in the real world. This means that it is time to discuss what in the heck a date is anyway. Cinderella had her godmother; we have the secret confessions of hundreds of suitors (and we're not out perpetuating lies and ruining romantic lives either). Karma and knowledge are on our side.

Now, to ensure you don't blow an evening out with a suitor who could be carrying your sparkly stiletto, you've got to learn the moves of the dance and know when to lead and when to follow, or else he might just waltz right out of your life before he even gives you a twirl.

Now, I know what you are thinking.

You are a smart, modern maiden who knows all there is to know about dating. You go out all of the time. You are charming and funny and can light up a room by just entering it. Not only do you not need to read this section, you could write it yourself.

Come close. *No, come a little closer.*

You're wrong.

Sorry.

I have been wrong, too.

We all have.

The one thing every prince, suitor, maiden, and toad have in common is a great big, fat, inflated ego. We love to believe that we know what is right and it's the *other gals* who have the long nasty hairs that need plucking. If this were true, you wouldn't be reading this book. So, kick off those mules and get comfy, because we're about to deconstruct the dating world!

What in the Heck Is a Date?

Here is what a date isn't: a night out with your boyfriend. A date with a suitor isn't a promise of anything; it's a subtle suggestion that there is a slight possibility that he is carrying a slipper in your size and that you might be comfortable wearing it. You are in the running for the crown—*along with dozens of other maidens.* A date is nothing more than a first step in a long, complicated courting dance, and one misstep can destroy the entire performance. His asking you out doesn't mean he's in love with you or that he's ready to sit under a tree and fill out a "compatibility test." It just means he thinks you and he could have a good time. That's about as deep as it gets.

While your fantasies have you dreaming about falling madly in love and having tea with the queen while he plays polo with your nephew, reality has something else in mind—something a little less grandiose and a lot less secure. So snap out of it, sister! Right now, he's thinking he might have a good meal and maybe he'll get a little nooky (which, if you like him, you won't provide him . . . but more on that later). This does not mean he's a toad. It just means he, like every other male out there, is under the spell of the penis.

Though Cinderella's version had the prince holding a ball to meet the woman he would marry, the truth is that princes, toads, and suitors alike all like to get laid, which is why it is their first and ultimate goal (but don't give in if you want that slipper!). Even the most sincere suitor does not go out looking for a wife every time he shares a goblet of wine or breaks some bread. He goes out looking to have fun with a variety of maidens, thinking that eventually one might surprise him and inspire him to commit.

This is the difference between our suitors and us. We maidens date because we are longing for love and looking for companionship. For us, dating might be a pleasant experience, but more often than not it is a means to an end. Our suitors see dating as a lot of fun, which will turn into something deeper when they have had their "aha!" moment (Chapter 3) and subsequently find a maiden they feel is worthy of their monogamy.

Common Mistakes We Maidens Make in the World of Dating

As you can see, the first date is only the beginning. So, before you start gushing to your mother, airing your dirty laundry, talking about yourself nonstop, or unpacking your emotional baggage, let's talk about some of the things you can do to give him the best possible impression of yourself. Remember, it's what you do long before the clock strikes midnight that will determine where the possible relationship will go.

After all, you might be the coolest maiden in all of the land, but your date may never know it if you spend the entire date worrying about what he thinks of you, pushing for a connection, or running down a list of questions you should have waited several dates to ask. Your first few dates are meant to establish if there is real chemistry and a connection, not to find out how much he owes on his student loans or discuss your issues with your mother. While it is extremely important that you present your authentic self and that you get to know more about him, there are limits to how far one should take it in the beginning. Here are some common mistakes we maidens have all made at one time or another, along with some helpful suggestions for navigating successfully through the dating maze.

We Are Addicted to Romance

If you are a little lover of love, you may be floating on cloud nine every time you meet a new suitor. However, you remain one blast away from emotional suicide as your constant anointment of devotion on the head of every common man you meet is a game of romantic roulette. You are so madly in love with the idea of love that by the time your waitress takes your drink order you have started to scribble your new initials on your napkins.

This is the maiden who believes wholeheartedly in fate (see later in the chapter). She spends a lot of time with astrologers who promise her that for a small fee, they can lift the romantic curse that has been bestowed upon her by a jealous relative or evil witch. If this sounds like you, consider this an intervention. Your idealism might be intoxicating, and your eyes sparkle all right, but it isn't love that's causing it. It's merely the thick glaze of self-deception. With all that gooey deception clouding your clarity, it's no wonder you claim you never saw the ever-present warning signs of incompatibility. By setting your heart on the idea that every new suitor is your prince, you leave yourself vulnerable and open to being used. Learn to take things slowly, and make it a point to see a lad for who he really is and not who you want him to be.

Real-World Suggestion Buy a journal and write out his dating review. Jot down things that were said and done throughout each date. Was he funny? Respectful? Did he ask you questions about yourself and your life, or did he yammer on about how important his job is? Don't write how happy you are to have met him or what your dreams are but what he said to make you laugh, what you found interesting about him, and anything he said or did that made you uncomfortable.

We Give Up Too Easily

We've all been there. Three bad dates in two weeks, and we've got Mr. "I-need-to-take-you-to-coffee-to-see-if-you-are-worthy-of-drinks—to-see-if-you-are-worthy-of-dinner" penciled in for tomorrow. You want to meet a good guy, so you dry-clean that great wrap dress, dash on your last ounce of faith, and resist the urge to cancel.

If you have ever been more willing to *swallow* a glass slipper than be without one another day, you're not alone. After all, there is a reason the singles bars are full of jopefuls (jaded hopefuls) on just about every night of the week and the online dating industry rakes in an estimated $500 million a year. Just about everyone is looking for love (or at least a little lovin'). It's not just you or even just you and your friends. It's a totally natural desire to want someone to ask you how your day was or remind you of the passion that can be found in a kiss. Everyone wants someone there to share their happiness, wipe their tears, and acknowledge their life has a purpose. The problem is we often forget that, even without this acknowledgment, our lives do have meaning, and the desire to win the dating game should be kept in perspective. Now, we all know doing that is about as easy as not giving in to our desire to pick up a toad's call just because we are lonely—but do it, we must.

Real-World Suggestion Date yourself until you have found someone you feel like dating! Take yourself out to great dinners with friends, get yourself a pedicure, and enjoy the perks of the life you have created and the joy of not having to answer to anyone. Take a look at my suggestions from Chapter 4 for more great ideas for enjoying single life.

We Believe in "the One" Instead of Many

According to worldometers.com, as of June 15, 2006, at 10:55 A.M. EST, there were approximately 6,569,524,953 people in all of the land. Now, call me a cynic, call me crazy, but please don't call me and tell me that my soul has just one mate! Neither does yours. Think about it. Do you really believe life is that screwed up? What if my guy is living somewhere in Milan? What if I find this out and he takes a trip to Rome the weekend I rush to Milan to meet him?

If this were the case, then most of us simply wouldn't have enough frequent-flier miles or vacation days to find true love. We'd all be screwed! So there might not be a guy in that particular bar on that particular night, but since when is that any indication there are not several or even dozens of wonderful suitors out there (yes, in your geographical area) ready to meet you?

Real-World Suggestion Realize that the idea of one match for every person may sound romantic in theory, but it's extremely limiting in practice and as unrealistic as flying horses.

We Hold onto Silly Ideals

You have always imagined yourself with a gorgeous Antonio Banderas look-alike with an accent and an estate in Spain. So you sit around daydreaming about his chocolate-brown eyes and sexy accent instead of accepting dates with one of the great-looking blue-eyed suitors who surround you in Perkiomenville, Pennsylvania.

Unless you want to live alone for the rest of your life, you have two choices: move abroad or give one of the good guys around you a chance. We all have fantasies about what our lives should, could, or will be like, but it's detrimental to dating to allow our daydreams to hinder our reality.

Real-World Suggestion If you are attracted to someone, he makes you smile, and you like his personality, don't cut him loose just because he doesn't live up to the ideal you always pictured yourself with. This isn't settling. It's having an open mind. You never knew you liked calamari until you tried it.

We Think We Can Change a Toad into a Prince

How many times have you been sitting with your girlfriends, listening to one of them go on and on with the same old complaints about a guy she is seeing? How many times have *you* done it? We stick it out in unhappy situations with lads who are a dozen bad habits away from being our prince; yet somehow we are surprised every time they do something to tick us off.

If changing yourself takes a lot of effort, wait until you try to change the inner workings of another human being you have known just a few years, if that. Just like running in slippers made of glass, it sounds easy enough, until you try it.

Real-World Suggestion Fixer-uppers are simply not great investments in the dating economy. Save your energy, love, and sanity, and put them in something that offers better returns. Take a look at Chapter 10 if you're not sure your guy is holding you back.

We Want a Flawless Relationship

Whether it's our hair, lips, little black ball gown, or prince, we have set some high standards. We want perfection, and we want it to go, thank you. Unfortunately, it's never going to happen. Sure it would be nice to have an unblemished life, but it's hard enough to get the ideal martini in the real world, and you're attempting to achieve perfection in a partnership and life? Seriously, woman, get a grip!

By now, you should be starting to understand that human beings don't come in flawless (otherwise I'd take mine well toned with extra empathy, loads of romance, and a flat in Soho on the side). Besides, when you think about it, perfection, like beauty, is arbitrary anyway.

The tale spun by Cinderella was done as a way of hiding her manipulation and the severe romantic issues she and her hubby had inside of the castle. I mean, think about it. This chick groaned and complained about her family, asked for favors from a fairy godmother, and hung out with cold-blooded people. Clearly, her story was about keeping face.

After causing such a commotion, would you admit that your so-called prince refused to pick up his socks, forgot your anniversary, and once pawned your tiara to pay off his polo wager? I think not. And so our dear Cindy opted to lie again. As far as anyone would know, her prince was perfect, handsome, and kind. He took out the trash and told her how gorgeous she was every morning. Her prince was totally made up, which means you've got to stop holding yours up to standards based on BS.

Now, you might know on an intellectual level that the perfect man does not exist, but have you really accepted that it is not feasible for a man to be all things at all times? Think about the things you want and ask yourself, "Would it be fair for him to ask me to live up to my own standards?"

The reality is that most maidens are so brainwashed by Cinderella's lie and the idea they should be living in a world of romance and ecstasy twenty-four–seven that they never give real suitors a chance. This is the reason they are sitting on their couches complaining while the lads in the world are moving about, enjoying life. With your heart in a fantasy and your being in reality, you are caught in an emotional tug-of-war that is destined to leave you exhausted and confused, which reeks havoc on the complexion, by the way.

Real-World Suggestion It's time to grab another piece of paper. Jot down all of the things you expect out of a partner. Are you looking for a funny, gorgeous, successful man or one who makes you giggle so hard you pee a little? Does he need to be romantic and tender, empathetic and kind seven days a week? Good luck, sister! Again, reality has limitations and flawlessness exceeds them. So, what's a gal to do? Why not give perfection a more realistic meaning. Here in the real world, perfection is based on the specific desires of each individual. This means that perfection is relative. What is perfect in your eyes might be less so in the eyes of another. This means that the cookie-cutter ideals that are limiting you should be tossed.

We Don't Understand That Fate Is Fatal to Dating

While they might be supremely romantic in saucy novels and romantic comedies, when you really evaluate their meaning, fate and destiny are nothing but two very sharp ends on a double-edged sword. The notion that life is preplanned and some maidens are destined to meet someone while others are destined to be alone is a wicked conclusion.

Look, gals. As much as a dry spell might make you believe you are "destined" to be alone, no maiden is born with a spell on her (despite what many sidewalk astrologers would like you to believe). We are all born with a clean slate. We may not have been born into the best family or situation, but once we are adults, we have the power and access to change our lives significantly. We can seek therapy, we can choose with whom to spend our time, and we set our own limits and boundaries in life. We are the ones who create our own successes, achievements, and connections by taking a proactive role in our own life. Don't accept the unacceptable; change the changeable. In many ways, fate is a cop-out. It allows us to sit on the sidelines and blame something bigger for our sadness, and when we do meet someone, we give credit to something other than ourselves. What about accepting the fact that your accomplishments and connections with people are because you have worked hard in life to be the best person you can be? You have taken the initiative to go out and meet people, and you have put yourself at the forefront of your life. While the idea of the universe bringing two people together can make us all sigh, it's an emotionally expensive theory to buy into. You will not bump into your prince sitting on your caboose waiting for destiny to bring him to your door. Remember, your life's carriage needs a driver, and you're the one who knows how to maneuver those horses. So take the reins because otherwise your romantic life is just going to sit there while dozens of other carriages pass you by.

Real-World Suggestion Toss the blueprint. Free will suggests that you have chances every day to shape your existence, so nurture your relationships with others and the one you have with yourself. Stop with the reactive number and do something out of the ordinary. Life is full of opportunities to meet new people and experience new things, and it's up to you to take them. No one is going to messenger happiness and love to your door. Sorry.

We Run Our Dates like Interviews

Does he want children? Where does he live? How much does he make? Does he brush his teeth before bed? What is the thread count on his sheets? Interviewing your date is not only boring but it can be annoying for the one being bombarded with questions. If you have ever been the maiden who sits down to dinner only to find yourself reciting a list of compatibility questions and blurting out your basic boyfriend job description, you've got to turn off the overhead light and stop the interrogation already!

Spending the entire evening reciting a list of likes and dislikes and asking the poor sap a boatload of questions will leave him about as comfortable as a rectal examination. Asking questions about someone is the way to get to know them, but keep it simple and light at first (such as asking about travel and his hobbies) before you try and find out if he has ever had skid marks in his knickers.

Real-World Suggestion Relax and allow things to unfold slowly like a wonderful plot in a good book. Savor getting to know him, and pay attention to how he acts and reacts and what he chats about. All of these things can be more telling than any quick-witted response he might give to one of your many questions.

We Expect Every Ball to Be Our Last

Despite what she might have put out through the palace PR rep, we now know that Cinderella married a lad without taking the time to get to know him or try on his slipper. Remember, this girl was in such a hurry to get hitched that she left her own slipper behind! Had she taken the time to attend a few balls, there is a very good chance she would have found a lad who would have taken her out, gotten to know her, and had much more in common with her.

The same will go for you. It is for this reason that it is imperative to take the time to attend several balls, dance with numerous suitors, and halt the expectation that every ball we attend will be our last. Every dance you participate in will not send you floating, and every lad you spend time with will not be a royal. Not accepting this will only chip away at your self-esteem. I know this will be hard to swallow, but sometimes it's OK to just have a good time.

Real-World Suggestion Expect that you will get something new out of every ball—it may be a new dance move, a new friend, or a wonderful new suitor. Hell, it might be that you learn you don't like the kind of music the DJ played. You don't always find the right ball gown at the first store, but that doesn't mean the dress is not out there. You just have to keep looking for it.

We Think We Get Only One Chance at Royalty

Sometimes we meet a great suitor and, before you know it, we're flaunting it all over town, sharing banana pancakes over brunch, having tea with the queen, and calling him "schmoopy" in public locales. Then, just as we get comfortable and start thanking our lucky stars for being swept off of our feet by this incredible lad, love takes a wrong turn and BAM! We get dropped right on our heads. What's a gal to do? Well, if you listen to Cinderella's schpeel you'll probably lock yourself in a tower somewhere and convince yourself that you'll never find a connection like the one you had with Mr. Swoop-n-Drop.

But you aren't going to do that, are you? Nope. Know why? Because you understand that sometimes love just does a belly flop. Instead of sinking to the bottom of the dating pool and drowning in your sorrows, you are going to ice that bruised ego, tape up that broken heart, and climb right back on that diving board. Always remember that some love is everlasting, some is fleeting, and some just fades over time. Unless you are stale and cemented in your ways, you will evolve over time, and so will others. The key is to learn from each mate (good and bad) and find the one who connects with you and is flexible enough to change along with you.

You are more than meets the eye, and so is your partner. You have different layers and a variety of interests that may change at any time. None of us is the same person today that we were ten years ago, and you will not be the same person ten years from now. This means that while one story may have led to a painful ending, it's a chapter in your book of life and a brick cemented into the bridge that will carry you to where you are going. It's not where you live.

Real-World Suggestion The truth is that just because this situation didn't work out doesn't mean that there aren't several royal babes out there capable of making you happy, appreciating you, and loving you. Just give yourself time, and remember, don't cry over anyone who is not crying over you.

We Campaign for the Crown

You're a catch. No really, you are! You are smart, sophisticated, and extremely successful. And in case he hasn't figured it out yet, you are going to let him know every chance you get. You think you are showing confidence, but he thinks you are as insecure as a starlet on her first audition. Verbalizing your "dateability" comes off as tacky as telling him how beautiful you think you are. Not only does it counterbalance any positive conclusions he may have come to about you, but it makes you sound desperate—as though you are campaigning for his affection.

Real-World Suggestion It's best to let your manners, charm, and style speak for themselves. Remember, actions really do speak louder than words. Besides, you don't elect a princess; you anoint her.

We Act as Though We Already Know Him

It's important to be yourself and be comfortable, but there is a difference between letting your guard down and letting it all hang out. So put your shoes back on, keep quiet about his ex, and get out of his refrigerator. Being comfortable on a date is a good thing, but acting as if you are old college buddies is another.

First, getting too personal and making comments about his life or likes can be taken as judgments and sarcasm. Teasing and offensive jokes can also backfire because you have no idea what his comfort level might be. Helping yourself to his personal belongings and checking out his medicine cabinet make you seem disrespectful and invasive (which, if you are doing this, you are). No one is saying not to have fun, but be cautious, and remember that you don't know this person.

Real-World Suggestion The best bet is to keep the conversation neutral and light and tell jokes you wouldn't be afraid to tell at a cocktail party with a friend's boss. Always wait until you've been invited to look through his photo album.

We Morph

Wait, where did your personality go? He likes tennis, you like tennis. He loves chardonnay; you toss your merlot and ask for a new goblet. The Morphing Maiden has an excellent ability to transform herself into whomever it is she thinks her date wants her to be. What she doesn't realize is that she is being deceitful and manipulative. She thinks she's being agreeable and, hey, she might find tennis a lot of fun someday!

A prince wants someone with whom he shares things in common, but watching a maiden turn into his clone is just creepy! In doing this, she might snag a prince, but it will be someone else's. The charade can last only so long, which means someone will wind up miserable. Either she'll feel suffocated, or she'll suffocate him trying to change him.

Real-World Suggestion If this is you, ask yourself why you are shoving your foot into a slipper that doesn't fit. Do you want blisters for the rest of your life? Don't you deserve the best possible match? Aren't your hobbies, likes, and desires important enough to share? Take some time to figure out who you are, and stay true to your uniqueness. It might be your differences that bring you together!

We Place Ourselves on Mute

You may be shy or you may just be a nervous wreck, but it really doesn't matter because he thinks you're about as exciting as a paleontology convention. With one-word answers and little nods, time together feels less like a date and more like an afternoon at the DMV. Let the agonizing and uncomfortable silences begin!

Real-World Suggestion If it's nerves that have paralyzed your tongue, take a minute to remind yourself that something about you made this chap want to get to know you better. You might as well show him your real personality because, so far, so good! If it is truly because you have nothing to say, well, maybe it's time to get a hobby. Fast!

We Don't Hold Ourselves Accountable

When a lad asks you out, it usually means that he has taken notice of your positive traits. However, like a beautiful linen tablecloth, you mustn't ruin its elegance and beauty by spilling your issues all over it. In doing so, you soil your chances of putting your fantastic traits on display, and don't you deserve to show them off? The best way to do this is to remain totally aware of yourself and your actions.

Many times, we maidens forget this crucial aspect of dating—we have total control over everything we say and do. No one can make us drink more than we should. No one can make us take the date to levels we aren't comfortable with. No one can force us to say things we don't want to say or to spill secrets that should be kept. This may all seem like common sense, but it's something we seem to forget at the most important moments.

More often than not, a prince's actions are simply reactions to something we are saying or doing. This means that we have far more control over a date and where it goes than we might realize. That's right, ladies, it's *you* that holds the power over the date. You are the ones setting the tone! Sure, he might take the lead in planning or conversation, but he's watching your reactions for clues as to who you really are and whether or not you are a good match for him. Do you engage him in conversation? Do you laugh at his jokes? Are you witty? What are your values and passions? Will you invite him in at the end of the evening or wait until you know him better? Will you get too tipsy and act like someone you're not, or will you carry yourself like the lady you are?

Real-World Suggestion Be yourself, but keep yourself under control. This is not your best friend, and he has no idea who you really are, which means his impressions will be cemented for the rest of the time he knows you. There are no second chances in dating.

We Try and Force It

While I'm sure Cinderella would love us all to believe that the prince was *so* intrigued with her that he went looking for her and married her as soon as he found her, this is nothing but our dear friend Cindy's wishful thinking. Sure she was his type, but the only reason she "fit his slipper" after the ball was because it was hers to begin with!

The truth is her prince was no prince at all. He was a confused little toad who hadn't a clue as to what he wanted other than a hot babe with a saucy dress and some shiny stilettos. This is clear because he went running after her (and married her) without knowing a damn thing about her! If only he would have taken the time to get to know about her anxiety disorder and she about his nasty little habit of not brushing his teeth for days at a time, maybe they wouldn't have had separate bedrooms. But that's another story. . . .

That slipper Cinderella tried on was her own, and it fit her foot. It was all about Cinderella's comfort with herself. Let me explain. Each suitor has traits that he is looking for in a mate. Some of it has to do with beauty and style, but a *real* prince also has a value system, ideals, passions, likes, and dislikes. He needs compatibility with his partner. This is what we call his "slipper" (which you read about in Chapter 3). If you are the maiden who can slip her saucy tootsies in there effortlessly, voilà! You've found your prince! He fits your needs, wants, and values, and you fit his.

Now, if each suitor has only one slipper on him at all times, then you don't have to be a math genius to understand that the odds of your fitting into the one carried by every lad on your dance card are low. This is why you shouldn't allow yourself to expect that every shoe will fit, or that you will want to wear it.

You might be attracted to a certain prince but find his sarcasm draining. You might like to lead while he expects you to follow. You may enjoy a blue blood's conversation but find the way he tortures your toes with his flawed quickstep terribly disappointing.

Real-World Suggestion Accept that despite what she might have put out through the palace PR rep, it's safe to assume that Cinderella had been to more than one ball and danced with more than one suitor before meeting her prince (and she was probably as frustrated as you are; hence, she left her own slipper behind). The same will go for you. I know this will be hard to swallow, but sometimes it's OK to just have a good time. Besides, remember that wearing the wrong shoe for days and days will just leave you tired, hurt, and utterly wicked!

We Believe in Love at First Sight

Is there anything more romantic than love at first sight? The notion of a cosmic connection is so powerful that every deep emotion we could feel comes surging up our spines, culminating in a dream come true all within a couple of minutes. It's damn well enough to make any maiden's heart flutter. Too bad there's no such thing, not even for our raven-haired heroine.

As I mentioned before, believing the story Cinderella told us would mean that her prince was actually a toad who cared only for her looks and her dress. Think about it: in any of the hundreds of versions of the tale, are there any mentions of a discussion between the two main characters? Does he know her favorite food or that she was allergic to shellfish? How about the fact that she hated polo, which was a passion of his? Of course not! There is simply no room for incompatibility in fairy tales. But beware: there is plenty of room for it here in the real world! In fact, there is so much room that it makes even the most handsome prince turn into an ugly old toad in the eyes of his once-adoring maiden.

Love at first sight suggests that love is based on looks. Unless you are Lady Superficial, you know that there's not much a maiden can count on when a lad bases his feelings on your hairdo, even if he's a loaded royal. The only things that pop up at "first sight" are chemistry, intrigue, and attraction. When you meet someone, everyone has got a clean slate. He has yet to show you the pile of dirty knickers under the bed or bore you to tears with his childish video game obsession, and you don't have foot fungus or an inability to pick your petticoats off of the floor. The only way to get to know someone is over time, and you have all of the time in the world, so take it.

Beware of any lad who acts as Cinderella's lad did. Any man who places that much effort into someone he doesn't know is not in love with you. He's got something else going on in his mind, and you shouldn't participate in his little dance. Cindy's story also suggests that you can learn all there is to know about someone in just a few minutes. Love is earned and built out of a connection, shared values and feelings, memories, and respect.

Real-World Suggestion Understand that sexual tension comes and goes, but love is earned. It grows, and it does not happen with a dance. Love is a culmination of a relationship, and a relationship takes more than a couple of weeks. If he is a prince—more specifically, if he is *your* prince—he'll want to get to know you properly, and everyone else will fade away. He'll ask you questions about yourself and will wait for you to open up to him on all levels at your own pace.

Tick, Tock—There Is No Clock (but Your Expectations Are Making You a Walking Time Bomb!)

Remember when you were a little girl with a birthday around the corner? The only thing you could think about was the events that were to take place on that special day. The whole day was to celebrate you with cake, presents, and your favorite friends. There were no worries about "getting older"; in fact, you embraced your new age with excitement and anticipation. A new year, a new you! There was no competition between you and your age until that one birthday. You know, the one where you suddenly felt a tiny surge of anxiety and pulled out your mental checklist of all of the accomplishments you should have achieved by now.

The next year, you felt it a little bit more. Before you knew it, you were doing whatever you could to avoid your yearly reminder of all of your perceived failures—especially those in the romance department. After the dinner with friends, you would go home and think about how those friends were all married or engaged and how the bars were getting old. Before you knew it, you were on your third piece of birthday cake, depressed on what was once your special day.

Real-World Suggestion Chill out! Despite Cinderella's confession that she snagged her man by midnight, there's no such thing as a clock or specific time in which you should have a prince or have created an heir. The very idea of there being a blueprint for life and love is a fantasy as full of bull as the one we are uncovering in this book. There is no time, age, or point in your life when you should be with someone until that point when you have met the right someone. The only clock that ticks is the one on the self-defeating time bomb that your expectations have put in your head. Let's deconstruct it before it blows up all of your self-esteem and ruins any chance of your finding happiness—alone or alongside your worthy royal (who is out there, by the way!).

We Keep Wishing Instead of Making Changes on Our Own

There is a story in which we all have a starring role—the one of overanalysis and self-defeatist talk. What starts out as a day of fun for us and our girlfriends quickly turns into a frustrating therapy session. Each of us takes our turn moaning and analyzing the actions of various lads none of us are able to understand. We make excuses, offer harsh judgments, and rub one another's egos, which leads to nothing but more thinking and a whole new set of concerns to discuss in next week's conversations. Doing this is not abnormal because we all do it. However, just because we've made it a habit doesn't mean it's healthy one, and it certainly hasn't proved productive.

If you have found that your brunches have started to taste a bit bitter, then it is time to sweeten things up a bit. You can do this by making a commitment to ending the neurotic and slightly insane pattern that is ruining your chances at seeing and accepting your prince. How do you do this? Well, it's a bit of complex magic known as changing your outlook, taking off the dark shades of negativity (or the ones with the rose-colored hue), opening your eyes, and becoming present in the moment in which you are living. The only way to seize the moment is to live in it by letting go of your past heartaches and daydreams of perfection.

This may sound easy, but I beg you, do not let its implied simplicity fool you into believing you won't have to make an effort. Start by walking down a familiar street and, for once, pay attention to the walk by not getting lost in your thoughts. Take a moment to notice every building you pass and look up! I promise you, you will see things that eluded you all of those hundreds of times before. You'll notice the intricacies of each shop and the height of the buildings.

Next, take a look at the city from a balcony or rooftop. Notice the lights and shadows, and take in the romance of the moment. This is what I want you to take with you when you walk back into the dating world. Remember the shock you felt at the new beauty and size of something you thought you knew. We are often so caught up in our own minds that we have no idea what is actually in front of us. This is why you have yet to find your prince! You cannot recognize him, and even if you do, on a subconscious level you aren't accepting him as your prince because he doesn't fit into the image you have in your mind. Therefore, you say and do things that ruin your chances with him.

Real-World Suggestion Taking full responsibility for your perceptions and becoming aware of your own reality without adding in black potions or white wishes will have a major impact on your actions. Moreover, changing what you put out into the world will have an impact on the way the universe and people in the world respond *to you*! It may sound a bit loopy, but you'd be amazed at just how much power you have over the way you experience your life and how others perceive you. You choose how you will prioritize your life and how you will handle yourself while living it. Will you see your goblet as half full or half empty? Will you mope around town with a puss on your face or see each day as a new opportunity to start over? The best part of grabbing ahold of the reins of your life is that you control where and when you go—no magic required.

We Date like Maidens

The difference between lads and maidens is that lads enjoy dating more. They understand that not every date will go well and don't put so much pressure on the evening to make it something it isn't. On the other hand, we maidens place so much emphasis on the night that we can actually destroy it. Our desire for a good partner has turned into a race to get the slipper on, never once ensuring that it fits! Like the ugly stepsisters, we squeeze and cry, shoving our hopes and dreams into something too small for our needs. This is not only a major turnoff for men but also detrimental to our emotional and mental health! By our actions, we are stating that our needs and desires are less important than having a man, and then we get angry at that man for not living up to the ideal of a prince.

Ladies, a prince is only a prince to the woman who is right for him. Every maiden's prince is another maiden's toad. Think about it. Remember that guy you really liked who broke your heart into a million pieces because he would not take you to dinner or commit and then married his next girlfriend and treats her like a princess? You spent hours sobbing that it was something about you, when really it was just that you were not the right match for him, and he was willing to accept it before you were.

Real-World Suggestion Before you can see the opportunity that lies in the single world, you are going to have to clean out the cinders in your mind, sweep out the ashes, and take a good look at the space without all of the hang-ups and piles of flawed thinking getting in the way. It is only then that you will be able to truly accept and embrace the blessing that is many nights with a variety of suitors with varying personalities, interests, hopes, dreams, and goals, which are all the better to choose from, my dear.

Helpful Tips for Having a Ball in the Dating World

- ~ **EAT!** Order something substantial, and enjoy it without telling him how worried you are about your growing bum.
- ~ **Bring your sense of humor.** You don't have to be a comedienne, but not taking yourself too seriously will make him take you more seriously.

~ **Turn off the cell.** There is nothing tackier than a maiden who interrupts her date to talk to someone else or "check who is calling." It leaves him with the impression that time with him is not as valuable as hearing from someone else.

~ **Be impressive by not trying to impress.** Don't throw your credentials at him.

~ **Turn down the heat.** Don't come on to him. Be flirtatious, but let him take the lead.

~ **Remember your manners.** Always thank him for a wonderful time, even if it wasn't.

Reality Check

Are You a Great Date, or Do You Suffer from Dating Behavioral Disorder?

1. Every dateable maiden knows that the best thing to wear on a first date is:
A. Something sexy, slinky, and cut up to there. You want to wow him with your gorgeous gams!

B. Something conservative to show him that you take yourself seriously and he should not expect sex—you are a respectable maiden.

C. Something comfortable and stylish but not over the top.

D. Jeans and a T-shirt—you're a laid-back girl.

2. *Makeup on a date should be:*

A. Glamorous and striking, like a night on the red carpet!

B. Extremely light and mostly in nudes.

C. Flattering; you highlight your best features and cover up little imperfections.

D. You don't wear makeup.

3. *Great date hair is:*

A. Washed and touchable, and it moves freely.

B. Blown out, teased, glossed, sprayed, and pinned.

C. Trendy: pigtails, berets, braids, or a side ponytail.

D. Pulled back in a ponytail.

4. *The best date conversations include:*

A. Deep, dark secrets about your crazy sister and wacky friend.

B. Friendly banter and a few jokes—where you went to school and what movies you have seen.

C. Biting sarcasm.

D. What your therapist thinks about your dating style.

5. *When drinking on a date, it's best to:*
A. Keep up with him so he thinks you are a cool chick.
B. Have a spritzer between glasses of wine because you are not a big drinker.
C. Order a round of shots for every round of drinks he buys.
D. Do body shots at the club!

6. *The hostess screwed up the reservation, the waiter messed up your order, and the busboy just spilled red wine on your pants. You:*
A. Smile through gritted teeth and silently eat your dinner.
B. Berate the busboy and demand to speak with the waiter. What is wrong with this staff?
C. Graciously accept the busboy's apology and the manager's offer to dry-clean your pants. Ask your date if he wouldn't mind stopping by your place so you can change.
D. Call it a night; your pants are ruined, your meal is cold, and you're miserable!

How did you do?

You are a great date if you chose the following answers:

1. **C.** You want to look attractive and as though you put in some effort, but you also want to be comfortable and not too over the top. Wear an outfit that is versatile and alluring, and do the sit-down test before you go out.

2. **C.** Again, you want to look like you take care of yourself and put in some effort but not as though you are wearing a mask or going to a job interview. Always perform the "natural light" test to ensure your makeup is light and flattering and not too orange/white/thick. On the other hand, if you really dislike makeup, dab a little mascara on your lashes, comb your brows, and wear a little clear gloss on your lips. Pinching your cheeks will give you a nice rosy flush.

3. **A.** A date isn't a baseball game, and it isn't an awards ceremony either. Keep your hair cleaned and polished, but avoid going overboard with anything too extreme, trendy, or cutesy. Think Jennifer Aniston, not Gwen Stefani.

4. **B.** Dateable maidens know that a date is all about a little chemistry and seeing whether there are things in common. Talking about personal demons will make him feel like a therapist (and that you need one), and mentioning that you have one will make him wonder what other issues you might have. Be personable but not too personal.

5. **B.** A dateable maiden knows her limits and that she is responsible for her behavior regardless of how much she has had to drink. Having a beer is fine, but if drinking two gives you the urge to dance on tables, you might want to sip the first one slowly. Besides, getting intoxicated on a date is a major turnoff for a prince. It shows him that you do not care about making a good impression, have no self-control, or, worse, want to use the alcohol as an excuse to do something you know is inappropriate. A toad, however, will love you—for the night.

6. C. How you handle a crisis and treat others is extremely important to suitors, and rest assured they are watching your every move. Maintaining your composure, treating people with respect, and making the best of the situation (and not taking it out on him or canceling the evening) will put you in a league all your own.

Chapter 6

The Lies We Speak into the Mirror

Y NOW WE know Cinderella's bloomers should have been in flames with all of her tall tales. But before we start throwing stones and setting up the guillotine, let us remind ourselves that we all have owned or at least rented glass cottages at one time or another.

Yep, that's right, gals. We are all guilty of fibbing our way through life, and this is nowhere more evident than in the area of our romantic lives. While the old saying may suggest that honesty is the best policy, it sure as heck never stopped a maiden from trimming the fat off of the truth to make it just a little more digestible.

You see, here in the real world we gals *love* to airbrush reality. Whether it's telling ourselves that the waistline of our favorite dress shrunk in the dryer or conveniently forgetting that we drank too much at the professional holiday ball, even the most earnest of gals can appreciate the art of a carefully applied little white lie.

We have become so accustomed to wearing our rose-colored specs that we have started to expect *others* to don them as well. We surround ourselves with friends who will promise us that our thighs don't look like two plump sausages in jeans three times too small. They assure us that a suitor's not calling us has something to do with his schedule or some accident his mother might have been in rather than the fact that we got loaded on the date and wound up drooling on ourselves in the cab. We want our friends to support our fantasy that every new guy is our insta-boyfriend or ignore the fact that we are talking about a lad we just met as though we have some kind of relationship with him.

The worst part in all of this is that we have become so accustomed to living in an alternative romantic universe that we get angry at any interruption the truth makes. If another maiden makes a comment about our corset being pulled too tight, we dub her "catty." If a suitor says he finds himself disinterested in pursuing a relationship with us after we've slept with him, we label him a superficial toad. Sometimes we gals *are* clawing at one another, and sometimes toads *do* find their way into our hearts. However, more often than not, we're the ones covering the mirror with cheesecloth in an attempt to soften what is staring back at us.

The Sweet Little Lie: Being a Bitch Is the Way to Gain Respect

Um, let's think about this for a moment: in order to have a healthy, empathetic, understanding relationship we are supposed to act bossy, nasty, nippy, controlling, and unattached? To impress someone you need to act unimpressed? This is supposed to show suitors that you are available and interested in them? How exhausting!

Why We Say It

Popular dating books and talk shows tell us that lads are destined to use, abuse, and walk all over us unless we toughen up. Girlfriends repeat this advice to one another without analyzing what kind of message they are choosing to perpetuate.

Cracking the Truth

Though they might be intriguing in prime-time soap operas, the truth is bitches suck. Do you want to date a jerk who allows little or no room for misunderstandings and doesn't accept your last-minute dinner suggestion out of fear you'll misinterpret his availability for weakness? Of course not! No matter how much these authors and television show producers try and dress up the phrase, the standard interpretation of the word *bitch* is universal, and it doesn't mean independent gal I want to spend time with. So please, let's all stop kidding ourselves.

Referring to yourself as a bitch carries some major implications such as proving that you don't know the difference between self-respect and rude behavior and that you believe relationships are about control and games. It says you don't mind being labeled one of the most derogatory names in the English language. How would you react if a lad and not another female called you this name?

Real-World Suggestion Be gentle but firm. Don't adhere to the idea that you have to play hard to gain respect. Be as kind, respectful, and flexible as you hope he will be, and live your life being true to your own personal value system. The truth is, being called a bitch is never a good thing. (If hanging out with your gay friends, disregard this whole section.)

The Sweet Little Lie: You Have to Play the Game if You Want to Win His Heart

There is a very big difference between allowing yourself to be disrespected and letting a potential royal know that it's OK to call you and that you are interested in seeing him again. After all, he is hoping you like him because he likes you. He's calling you because he wants to spend time with you.

Why We Say It

We are bombarded with messages through the media, movies, literature, and one another. We're told that lads will not respect you if you call back too soon, if you accept his date too late, or if you let him know you are not seeing anyone else.

Cracking the Truth

Why miss a chance to enjoy a movie with a guy you like just because he called and asked a day too late (or even the day of)? Uh, in my book, that's called spontaneity! Calling to see if you want to grab dinner after work is a lot different from calling you late at night and asking you to take a cab over to his pad to kiss his nether regions.

The important thing is for you to know what you are looking for, know what your boundaries are, and respect the boundaries he maintains. Be authentically you, and for goodness sakes, accept his dates regardless of when he asks you out (as long as they are respectful and not always in his apartment). Return calls at a normal rate (don't call ten times in a row because that's just weird), and be appreciative of his efforts. Trying to play emotional battleship will absolutely sink your chances with a good guy.

Real-World Suggestion This isn't chess; it's dating. The only game a prince likes is polo . . . maybe.

The Sweet Little Lie: I'm Not Acting Crazy!

While no one is denying you have a right to be heard, when it involves a vortex of flying feelings and false accusations, it's an emotional rights violation. It's best to figure out your emotions and where they stem from before you start bombing someone else's life with them. The idea that anyone unwilling to put up with irrational behavior is an unsympathetic toad is unfair and inaccurate.

Why We Say It

In this touchy-feely, blame-it-on-your-parents society, it's easy to believe that our feelings matter more than logic, healthy behavior, and rationale. If we feel a lad is doing something to wrong us, we have brainwashed ourselves into believing it condones loony behavior such as staking out his house, breaking into his e-mail, calling his friends to check up on him, or bursting into an emotional cloud of chaos.

I am not suggesting you not express yourself, but if your feelings are swaying from one extreme to another and your way of expression involves forcing a suitor to decode bits and pieces of crazy talk thrown at him via fifteen voice mail messages, you might need to settle down. This is especially vital when he has made it clear he does not wish to discuss them with you. While you might think you are just "being honest" and are "not playing games," the reality is that when it comes to weaving in and out of romantic situations, most of us are a bunch of basket cases.

Cracking the Truth

Infatuation and lust can be intoxicating, and for many of us, the fear of rejection can be so intense that we will do anything to prevent ourselves from feeling its nasty little sting. Unfortunately, this combination of highs and lows is enough to make anyone act a little loco—even you. According to Cinderella, logic has no place in romance, but where we live, we have to make room. If you find yourself stalking him, harassing his friends, calling him twenty times a day, or screaming out "I love you" after knowing him three weeks, he's right . . . you have gone a little loco. If you show up at his place uninvited, ignore his decision to break things off, or try and convince him to stay with you by creating a big emotional drama, I promise you, he's going to start fearing you are a rabbit boiler.

Real-World Suggestion Please remember first that you are accountable for every word you say and action you take, regardless of how upset you might be. Second, remember that you are being judged by these men, and judgments can come down so hard that they can destroy chances at a future with a good guy (even if it was a misunderstanding). A good rule to follow? If it doesn't sound sane in other parts of your life, don't bring it into your relationships. Example: if you wouldn't normally fake pregnancies to friends, obsessively analyze your boss, or scream and freak out on your neighbor, don't do it to him. Oh, and if you would, drop this book and get thee to a psychiatric care unit quickly!

The Sweet Little Lie: He Is a Toad for Sleeping with You and Not Calling

This is a lie I hear perpetuated by maidens throughout the land on a constant basis. It's time to swallow the cold, hard reality that is this: there is no connection between love and sex unless the lad decides to connect them. Unless he was calling you, inviting you to dinners, showing you respect, and pursuing some kind of relationship with you before you played the naked game, what in the world gave you the impression he would be doing these things afterward? Sex is an action, not an emotion, and tender gestures are motivated by feelings, not the horizontal mambo.

Why We Say It

What gal wants to admit to herself that she slept with someone before she got to know him and convinced herself that she mattered to him more than she did? That's no fun. Still, sleeping with someone is sex, and sex doesn't require respect the way love does.

Cracking the Truth

Let me break it down this way: say you are out at your favorite restaurant and the owner comes over and tells you to order the most expensive thing on the menu. He says it's on the house because he likes you so much and appreciates you being there. Now, when the bill comes, you might feel a little uncomfortable, but would you pay for the full meal or just tip? The next day, would you be thinking about and telling friends about the owner instead of the meal? No. He might get a mention, but you're stoked you got free filet mignon and champagne.

To a suitor, the idea of sex is fantastic, and chances are, he's not going to turn it down, but don't start thinking it means you can start borrowing his favorite sweatshirts just because you kissed his nether regions. It wasn't part of the trade. Everybody loves freebies. It's up to you to make him aware of any fine print beforehand. He's only a toad if he pretended to feel things he didn't. Did he lie, or did you tell yourself he felt a certain way or add meaning to something he said or did without letting him know?

Real-World Suggestion Accept this simple truth: sex is just sex. It's not love, and it never will be. Sex does not lead to love most of the time, and here is the most shocking part of all: With the exception of just a few, all of the men interviewed for this book agreed that you don't even have to like a maiden to have sex with her. One claimed he could even hate a woman and sleep with her! Ouch!

The Sweet Little Lie: You Must Analyze His Actions to Uncover His Real Feelings

We might believe that men are from another planet or are difficult to understand, but they aren't. That's just a bunch of candy-babble we tell ourselves to make ourselves feel better. The truth is, we just have to listen to what his words and actions tell us and believe him when he tells us who he is. It's time to stop stroking our egos by telling ourselves he is busy, shy, or playing hard to get.

Why We Say It

Obsessing about lads, love, relationships, and marriage have become stereotypical attributes that we gals have decidedly made habits. Romantic comedies endorse the idea of the neurotic female, and reality shows have several to dozens of maidens competing and biting at one another for the attention of one lad. These maidens always have to analyze the guy's actions and reactions with one another and usually work themselves into an anxiety attack by round three.

Then, of course, there are hundreds of dating books and magazines that are filled with long-winded analyses that try and explain what is behind everything from what your suitor says and does to how he sleeps and dresses. With all of this reinforcement, it's hard to take anything he says or does at face value. It's really not that complicated.

Cracking the Truth

Though we give them a lot of power, the truth is our suitors are neither mystical creatures nor do they speak in a top-secret code that needs to be analyzed and studied in order to be cracked.

No matter how much you want to throw him on a pedestal, he is a person just like you. The only power anyone has is the power you give them. Most of the time these lads are unaware of how worked up and stressed out you are. What's more is that he is a less complex person than his female counterpart. Want proof? When is the last time you heard about two men getting into an argument over the "real meaning" behind what he said in passing last Tuesday? If a lad likes you, you'll know. You'll feel good about the progress of the relationship, you'll feel respected, and you'll be spending time with him doing various activities and getting to know him, his friends, and his family. Furthermore, he'll be interested in getting to know the people and interests in your life. If you're analyzing, you might be overthinking, but most likely, you're just with the wrong guy.

Real-World Suggestion Don't work yourself into a tizzy going over various scenarios you and your friends have come up with. Don't take too many people's advice about what you should do or should have done or what he's thinking, should do, or should have done. Always remind yourself that if you have to think and think about it, he's not really thinking about you. Don't waste your time or break your own heart. Move on.

The Sweet Little Lie: We'll Be Great Once He Changes (Insert Habit Here)

As nice as this might be, it's not going to happen, and here is why. Each and every one of us is a product of who we have been, what we have experienced, and the millions of thought processes we have had since birth. We're a culmination of every second we have experienced until this very moment. What does this mean? What seems like a small effort in your eyes may well be a habit or trait that is cemented into the foundation of who he is as a human being, and change of any kind can be difficult.

Why We Say It

We want him to change! We believe our relationship will be fabulous when he changes, and it wouldn't be so difficult to make such a small effort, right?

Cracking the Truth

Making the decision to change your hairdo can be a terrifying experience, and you want to take on his psychology? See "I'm

Not Acting Crazy," because if your answer is yes, you are. Think about the habits and traits you have that you are interested in changing. How difficult is it to quit smoking or get yourself to the gym every day?

At least you are in full control of yourself, and—one hopes— you know your inner workings, demons, and motivations. Now, are you going to tell me that you are going to tackle the huge task of getting into someone else's mind, reworking the wires that have been there twenty, thirty, or more years, and getting him to change his core?

Real-World Suggestion Remember that he's a person, not a hair color.

The Sweet Little Lie: He May Not Be a Prince, but at Least I Have a Toad!

This lie is usually spoken once we have allowed our insecurity or loneliness to get the best of us. We convince ourselves that having the affection of a man will somehow fill in the cracks that are caused by everything that is missing in our lives. We tell ourselves that once we have a man, our crappy job won't bring us down, our social life will sparkle, and we won't be out of shape because we would have less reason to devour an entire bag of chocolate-covered peanuts on a lonely Friday night. Every bad thing in our world is attributed to our not having someone to share it with. Our happiness will remain far away if we stay stuck in this skewed version of reality.

Why We Say It

You are tired of dating and interested in having someone. For some reason or another you have concluded that it is better to have the attention of any ol' toad rather than to remain alone until you find your prince.

Cracking the Truth

Putting up with disrespectful behavior or staying with someone who doesn't fulfill you is like devouring a bad apple because you are too hungry to hold out for a crisp, tasty one. Not only is it unpleasant, but it can also make you sick! No one is saying you have to love being single, but a few lonely nights is nothing compared to a lifetime with the wrong mate. Remember, the slipper needs to fit, or you'll have to endure the pain of walking in a relationship that doesn't fit properly.

Real-World Suggestion Kissing toads will never bring you a crown, despite what you might have heard about your having to kiss a lot of them in order to meet your prince.

The Sweet Little Lie: When a Toad Continues to Hurt You, It's All His Fault

If a toad has worked his magic spell on you, that's not your fault. It happens to the best of us. But all of that should change once the spell has started to wear off and you have caught a glimpse of his warts.

Why We Say It

When Cinderella was growing up, a maiden had little control over her life. What she did, where she lived, and who she could and could not marry were all dictated by a society that viewed us as the less significant gender. However, in these modern times, we hold a much greater power over our lives, which allows us the ability to choose who we see, who we kiss, and who we toss back into the pond. Never forget, you control who is in your life.

Cracking the Truth

It might take a little while, but a toad will always leave you clues as to who he is (see Chapter 10). It's up to you to pay attention and not convince yourself he's something that he isn't! He may not come right out and say it, but he can hide his slimy backbone for only so long before you start seeing clues that he is more reptile than royal. It is then you who has the choice. You can cut your losses and tell him where to hop, or you can buzz around him like a little fly, convincing yourself that you can change him until he swallows you whole. If you choose the latter, you must remember that it was your choice to stay, which makes all of the pain, chaos, and frustration your responsibility, not his.

You are choosing to stay with him in spite of the pain he is causing you. Because we have learned that no amount of kindness, wishing, analyzing, or long-winded conversations will ever change someone with a transparent moral fiber, you have to change your tolerance level and walk. You simply cannot wish a square peg into a round hole.

Real-World Suggestion Remember what we have learned here: the only thing you'll get from kissing this toad is a big ugly wart. If you are trying to convince yourself otherwise, the joke is on you, and the only person you have to blame for it is yourself.

The Sweet Little Lie: You Must Be Perfect to Capture the Heart of a Prince

Cindy's long, lithe figure and shiny black hair might have caused her particular guy to dub her the most beautiful belle at the ball, but that was his personal preference. His brothers and cousins might find they are attracted to voluptuous redheads or petite blondes. In the end, it comes down to the unique charisma of each particular woman. Telling yourself that every maiden must look one particular way to "snag her prince" is silly, self-defeating, and totally inaccurate. It's also a cop-out. I want you to reread that sentence again and again until it becomes your mantra.

Why We Say It

In almost every version of Cinderella's story, it's suggested that even while covered in ashes and rags, our maiden was truly a sight to behold. Her natural beauty glowed and could be outshone only by her pure, gentle heart. Now, while Cindy might have cleaned up well, the idea that every man in all of the land could find her to be the most attractive maiden on the dance floor is difficult to swallow. If beauty truly is in the eye of the beholder (and I believe it is), then it's arbitrary and random and cannot be defined. Not everyone likes strawberries—no matter how gorgeous and tasty they might look.

Cracking the Truth

No certain size, shape, eye color, hairdo, or eye shadow will guarantee you the crown. Think about those sisters all dolled up and alone at the ball.

Now, this doesn't mean you can walk around in sweats with no makeup every day and assume your prince will notice you. You've still got to put in the effort! Take the time to highlight your unique features, and try and put your best face forward, smile and all. Taking care of yourself by cleaning up, exercising, eating well, and taking your vitamins will make you feel good on the inside. When you feel comfortable in your own skin, you radiate a confidence that throws a soft light over all of your features, accenting your spirit like flickering candles. Just be authentically you. Don't follow trends that you don't want to follow. Wear clothes that are flattering and fit well. There is nothing more gorgeous than a woman who knows herself and stays true to who she is.

Real-World Suggestion As I said, beauty is arbitrary. You don't have to look like Christy Turlington to find love, but feeling ugly inside will keep you feeling lonely.

Sweet Little Lie: A Prince Wants to Save You

Cinderella, many older relatives, and the authors of various dating books would like you to believe that the only way to find a man is to play the damsel-in-distress role. However, the truth is a prince is far more interested in finding a strong partner capable of her own decision making and able to formulate an opinion of her own. This means he is looking for someone to complement him and support him as he will support and complement her.

Why We Say It

As I mentioned before, in the days of Cinderella (and too long after) we were considered to be the weaker gender—prone to a life of menial housework and lipstick dabbing—thus eradicating any chance for survival or excitement without the help of a heroic prince to slay our dragons. This strong, virile man would prove his masculinity by saving poor, incapable us from the big, bad world.

Cracking the Truth

These days, we maidens are running companies and saving lives while our metrosexual princes are out having their eyebrows waxed and stealing our Potion Number Nine. Princes might like to feel strong and capable, as we do. However, the idea of having to swoop in and live your life for you by making all of your "big" decisions and saving you from your bad ones is a total turnoff and outright exhausting!

Just as we maidens do not want to have to "raise a partner," neither does a prince. What does this mean? Cultivate your own interests, take care of your own affairs, and indulge in your own hobbies. Own your life. It is a fallacy that strong men are intimidated by intelligent, capable maidens. In fact, it's quite the opposite. They are impressed and intrigued by them. Now, this is completely different from a toad who might want you to sit pretty and silent or be intimidated by your success or even your beauty, but do you really want to be treated like a statue?

Real-World Suggestion A maiden who places her life in the hands of anyone—royal or no—is setting herself up for a lifetime of bad potions and happy endings gone wrong. The only person who should "save" you is yourself.

The Sweet Little Lie: My Guy Is No Prince

OK, so, he doesn't bring you flowers daily, and the last time he helped you with the laundry was before washing machines were invented. Does that really make him a toad? No, it makes him human. The idea that your man is a prince only if he makes grand romantic gestures or helps you scrub the toilet is the lie that can be the most damaging to us, to him, and to our chances of recognizing what we have before we lose it.

Why We Say It

While in theory we all know that no one is perfect, there are times when a lad is unfairly judged simply because a maiden refuses to accept that her expectations are based on what she has read in storybooks and seen on television. When her guy falls short of her unachievable ideal, she berates him in her mind and compares him to the image of what she feels a royal should be. It becomes a vicious cycle that can tear away at even the most loving relationship.

Cracking the Truth

If you are finding yourself creating romantic obstacles for your man to overcome, there's a good chance you're slaying your chances at everlasting love. Just as you are your own unique individual, so is the man with whom you are sharing your time. He's not made up of characteristics on a checklist, and he's not a hero from a children's tale or a character in a movie. Instead, he is a flawed, complex, unique human being—just like you.

Imagine if he wanted you to act like a demure housewife when you are a vibrant career maiden, or if he asked you to act silly and ditzy because he found it charming when women did that on television. Maybe you don't show up at his house in lingerie, but does that make the dinners you cook and the Advil you bring when he is sick any less special? By reiterating your desire for your own "perfect man," you devalue the things he does do for you—all the while undermining his self-esteem and making him feel totally unappreciated. The more he feels pigeonholed, the higher the wall of resentment will be, and the less he will feel compelled to demonstrate his love for you.

Real-World Suggestion He may not sweep you off of your feet like Rhett did with Scarlett, and he might think ordering in constitutes a dinner date. However, if he makes you laugh, respects you, communicates with you, and cherishes you, he is very much a prince.

Royal Revelations:
Lies Exposed

"He's not thinking about the relationship most of the time. Women become obsessed, and men just kind of go with it."

—FRED, THIRTY, SAN FRANCISCO, CA

"What am I looking for in a girlfriend? I want someone who is not looking to change me drastically. If, when they met me, they knew I surfed and enjoyed surfing and a more laid-back lifestyle, then don't expect me to drop surfing, play dress-up, and go to a bar when we start dating."

—MIKE, THIRTY-THREE, SAN DIEGO, CA

"Women overthink everything and drive themselves insane; it makes me crazy to even listen to it."

—CHARLIE, TWENTY-EIGHT, LOS ANGELES, CA

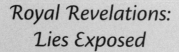

Chapter 7

———◆———

One-Night Stands
(and Other Bad Potions)

HAT DO YOU get when you mix one part saucy maiden with two parts horny prince, throw in a dash of conversation and a sprinkle of alcohol, and then mix it in a huge bowl of naked? One tasty batter, but try and bake it and watch it explode.

Cooking up a one-night stand is hardly the recipe for romance, but who are we kidding here, most people have tried to curb their appetites by licking the bowl du stranger at one point in their lives. Gorging on random sex can be fun, but it usually leaves you with a stomachache, regretting you didn't hold out for a decent dinner.

Whether it's because a maiden is looking for love, too tipsy to think straight, or lonely and in need of a pair of arms around her, there's something she's sure to find out after the act: getting busy with a stranger is strange business. While the practice of nude introductions is common throughout the land, it's a rarity that we ever find a prince who winds up dating—let alone marrying—such a conquest. It may sound old-fashioned and totally outdated, but maintaining a little self-control in the sex department is a timeless practice that offers numerous benefits to all parties. This is where Cinderella got it right. She knew when to call it a night and how to get a suitor to come looking for more.

OK, so she had very little choice in the matter lest she wish to return to her rags in front of her cute new beau, but for many a maiden, resisting the charm of both the moon and a suitor with a six-pack can prove more difficult. Most of us would be willing to get out of those rags long before he ever caught wind of our little secret.

Why Do We Do It?

I am sure there are a million psychological reasons that can explain why we hop into bed with Mr. Saucy, but I'm going to stick with the basics. There are, of course, the most common reasons: loneliness, alcohol, sexual attraction, and the desire to have a good time. But there's something more.

I daresay, blame it on the moonlight. There's a mutual understanding among most of us that what happens between the hours of sundown and dawn is exempt from all consequences. The night provides a soft, romantic glow that airbrushes all questionable judgments. I mean, think about it, there is something magical about the soft light of a starry sky, the romance it sprinkles on all who walk beneath it. Balls, dinners, first kisses, and cocktails are all usually scheduled on the clock of the evening, and this is no fluke, be sure! It's for this reason that we must understand the night's power and allow it to work to our benefit—without allowing its influence to ruin our chances with our royal.

We may have once believed that kissing the right toad will yield us a prince, but now we know differently. Kissing a suitor will send you floating. Kissing a toad might be fun for some time, but in the end, it'll just lead to overanalysis and leave you open to the possibility of a broken heart and a bad case of warts! YUCK.

Double Knot That Corset and Lock That Chastity Belt!

Snap out of it, gals! No matter how liberated a society you might think we live in, the cold, hard truth is that sleeping with a lad too soon is not going to win you any points. You can sit and protest this annoying double standard, or you can realize that just because the boys don't get labeled for it doesn't mean they shouldn't! The fact of the matter is that sex and love are two different things, and the only thing that will link them is respect—and that's not coming your way if you're dropping knickers after a couple of beers. Truth be told, we maidens should hold the same view as the boys do about us. If he's willing to be inside you before he even knows your last name, he's not exactly Mr. Fabulous. He's a horny toad looking for a cave to crawl into. Not very romantic, is it?

No matter how unfair it is, how much these guys claim they don't buy into it, or how much you try and convince yourself you don't care about it, a suitor doesn't feel the same way about you after a one-night stand. That's just reality.

Sleeping with a lad too soon may not make him think less of you as a human being, but that doesn't mean he's going to date you. Why would he? You have already shown him your goodies, and he's fairly certain your willingness to do so means you've done it before. He thinks you're an easy lay (because you were), and you should think the same thing about him (because he was). He might call you again and he might not, but, if he does, there's a good chance it won't be for anything other than a roll in the sack. A dog will always come back to the house that gave him a free steak.

What Men Are *Really* Thinking

It may be a harsh reality, but it's very real, so pay attention. This information didn't come from my own personal moral convictions. It came straight from the mouths of the suitors themselves, and I spoke to nearly a thousand of them.

Nearly all of the suitors polled for this book claimed that while they might be begging, pleading, and plotting to get your petticoat off, giving in and taking them back to your cottage for some passion à la mode on the first couple of dates rates as the number one way to ensure you will not be asked to another ball—let alone for your hand. More shocking was the admission by suitors and princes that a maiden's decision to sleep with him too early put a spell on him that might actually make him act like a toad toward her! That's right! Perfectly decent men will act in ways they normally don't as a reaction to a maiden not respecting herself enough to hold out for more! Cinderella may have had ulterior motives for rushing home when the clock struck twelve, but that's not the point. The bottom line is that she did it, and that makes all of the difference in the world.

Now, for those maidens out there who enjoy a more modern view, you might be thinking this is hogwash, that you are both consenting adults, blah, blah, blah. Zip it. He will think you are easy, and no man wants to commit to an easy woman, not long term at least.

While enjoying the carnal pleasures of a randy royal might indulge you in the dark, by now we all know how uncomfortable the walk of shame (jumping into a carriage/cab in old makeup and last night's gown) can be. There's something about the bright judgment of the sun that can melt the strongest wall of confidence. You might leave his place wondering if he will call and recounting details with your girlfriends on your cellie, but he's showering and glad to have you gone. Sure, the night before, he couldn't wait to get you home, but this morning he was counting the minutes until you left. It's called regrets.

What You Are *Really* Thinking

There's a reason you worry if he thinks you are easy when you sleep with him too fast. Deep down you know he does because you were! They may love sex, but lads feel the same judgments we do when they leave the cottage of someone they barely know. Unfortunately, as soon as the saucy sex session is over, reality sets in. The reality is that you don't know one another and he's been inside of you. Regret ensues and somehow gets weaved in with your image. He's grossed out. He's wondering if you have anything. He's showering and glad to be going back to his life. He's got all kinds of misconceptions about you. How do I know this? A suitor told me this verbatim.

A good guy doesn't want to be a toad in the daylight or view the maiden he chooses to be with as a harlot. He wants a princess, and in his eyes, a princess respects herself enough not to drop dress at first night. She knows she is worthy of meeting out in the daylight for a walk, coffee, or brunch. She knows she deserves more than a roll in the hay. No matter how much he states to the contrary in the evening, no lad wants to know where your saucy freckle is before he knows that you despise sports and live for the perfect slice of banana cream pie.

So, while his chest might be screaming for you to kiss it and his lips might beg to come in, the only way you're ever going to get more than just a kiss is to wait to do more than kiss. This goes for even the most respectable maiden in all the land. If you do it with him once, in his mind, it's as good as doing it with everyone, because he'll think you have.

Still not convinced? Look at it this way. Sleeping with a suitor too soon is like pressing the fast-forward button on the relationship DVD. In doing so, you accept that you will never get to watch the plot unfold or take in the lovely cinematography you would surely have enjoyed. You accept that your attraction and desire to spend thirty minutes (and that's if you are lucky!) rolling around is worth rushing to the end. Once you get there, there's nowhere else to go. It's over. Is it worth rewinding when you've spoiled the finale? The bottom line is that should you choose to have a one-night stand, chances are it'll be fun, but you won't be meeting Grandma.

As one suitor put it, "If you want to have a one-night stand, do it, go for it! Just don't expect a phone call unless he forgot something at your place, and even then, that could be written off by them as a cost to doing business." Eek!

Take a look at some other bad potions guaranteed to kill your chances with a suitor and any chance of trying that slipper on for size.

Bad Potion: Drunk Dialing/ Texting/E-Mailing

Your fairy-tale take: You've been out all night with your best girlfriends and suddenly that song comes on. You know, the one that totally reminds you of the suitor you're vibing? You dig through your pocketbook and grab your cellie. After a few screwups on the keypad, you manage to get through to Mr.

Fantastic, who is watching late-night reruns of "The Sopranos" in his apartment. Innocent call to let him know you're thinking about him, right? Wrong. Oh, so very wrong.

Reality: You're drunk. You're not in control, and your words are swishy or terribly misspelled, I promise. There is nothing attractive about a grown woman screaming into a phone from a club when you are sitting in your silent apartment in your pajamas. Heaven knows what you are saying! Oh, and being tipsy is no excuse, so stop using it as one to tell him you love him or want to have his baby. Remember what you learned about dating? You're accountable for everything you say and do. If you murder your reputation with your suitor, being loaded is not going to be a decent enough defense to get you off of the hook.

Real-World Suggestion Write his number down and leave it at home. Delete it out of your cell phone before you leave, or simply give your phone to a trusted friend.

Bad Potion: Calling Too Much

Your fairy-tale take: You like him. I mean, you really like him. The great news is he really seems to like you, which is why you're sure he doesn't mind your calling him three times in two hours after knowing him a month and a half. After all, you just want to make sure you are still on for dinner tomorrow. Not a bad idea, right? Wrong.

Reality: Calling him too often makes you seem overeager at best and controlling at worst. Depending on the situation, your suitor may be turned off by your lack of self-control or worry that if you're like this when dating, how far up his bum will you ride when you're exclusive?

Real-World Suggestion Show him you have your own life by living it and not having so much free time that you need to hear his voice every thirty minutes. Not only will he appreciate your independence and the respect you show him by appreciating his, you will most likely have more of his attention, as he will wonder what is so great in your life that you aren't acting like most of the insecure, controlling women he's dated!

Bad Potion: Crazy E-Mailing

Your fairy-tale take: It's been bottled up inside of you too long. You need to explain your feelings to him. You need to know where this relationship is headed, and if it's not headed to the land of exclusivity, things need to change. It's time he knows how you really feel.

Reality: He thinks things are progressing nicely and at a normal pace, and he loved seeing you last night! He's sitting at work, sipping his coffee, and noshing on a dry bagel when his in-box lights up. He clicks it and BAM! A bunch of psychobabble explodes all over his screen. There's nothing less appealing than an overemotional, long-winded e-mail popping into your in-box while you're working on that presentation for your boss. Oh, and don't kid yourself. He's going to forward that to his friends and ask his female coworkers what they think about it.

Real-World Suggestion Save e-mail for work and catching up, not for serious issues that need to be resolved in person. E-mail is not fail-proof (ever send an e-mail to the wrong person?), and it's often read by third parties when at work. Even worse, you have zero control over the way he takes your tone, and you can never take it back.

Bad Potion: Getting Too Friendly with His Friends

Your fairy-tale take: You've been out with him and his friends on several occasions. One has taken a liking to you, offering you advice, taking your coat, and buying you cocktails. He's always talking you up to your suitor and tells you all of the wonderful things your guy says about you when you're not around. You begin to believe that he is a friend separate to you. This is a fatal mistake.

Reality: There are two things that could be happening here, and neither of them benefits you, love. The first is that his friend wants to get into your pants (which makes him a despicable toad), and the second is that he's trying to get his friend laid and show you a good time while you're around. Don't kid yourself into believing that this person will keep your secrets or tell you anything your suitor doesn't want you to hear. Besides, your suitor may find this new "chumminess" uncomfortable or start to think you're being manipulative. Plus, you have no control as to how your words will be revealed to your suitor or if they will even be the ones you uttered.

Real-World Suggestion Be courteous and friendly, but keep your conversations light. Confide in your friends and your diary, and keep the questions about him for him.

Bad Potion: Coming on Too Strong

Your fairy-tale take: You've watched Demi in *Disclosure* and Sharon in *Basic Instinct*, and you've heard the rumors about Angelina. Characters on popular cable shows sexually harass lads in every episode. You don't play games! Forward is sexy. Forward is dangerous. You say what you mean, and if they can't handle a mature maiden like you, screw them!

Reality: In actuality, forward is kind of frightening because it leaves very little mystery and speeds everything to a halt. Just like in the one-night stand (which is the physical manifestation of this behavior), acting forward is hardly the way to find a great guy. There's no buildup. While a toad looking for a quick bed hop may love your direct ways, a suitor will find your immodesty a total turnoff. Tying that cherry string, telling him that you'll be the best lay of his life, or informing him that you're dying to bathe him with your tongue may sound great in your head, but when the words fly off of your lips, a lad hears the sound of a maiden who uses her body and sexuality as bait. And asking him where the relationship is going a week after meeting him is just the actions of a crazy woman. An easy score is boring, and no matter how much you try and tell yourself you're liberated, sexy, and free, being bold only means that you're bold.

Real-World Suggestion Expressing yourself in such a harsh manner is about as flattering as holding a "Just Do Me" sign under a neon light. Unless you've created the kind of relationship (over time) where you both are comfortable with communicating in this manner, it's best to hold back and think about how he might react to such statements. Do you know enough about him? Is he conservative?

Is he shy? Think about your actions, and remember that you are accountable.

Bad Potion: Meeting Him Out or at His House Late at Night

Your fairy-tale take: You've seen him a couple of times and you'd have gone out with him for dinner, but he had his friend's birthday party, and tonight he had to work late. He's off Saturday, but it's Friday and he really wants to see you! You both seem to like one another, and you've been texting all night. He calls you from the restaurant and invites you over to his place. He even offers to pay for your cab—so sweet! Alas, no it isn't.

Reality: OK, ladies, let's be real here. Most of the time, if a lad wants to spend time with you he will have the courtesy to call you before 1:00 A.M. More often than not, this behavior suggests that he went out with his friends looking for women and when he didn't score, he called his "sure thing," which is you. Now, if you're dating a lad who normally treats you well and he suddenly picks up this habit, you can be sure he's a suitor testing your boundaries (and, of course, looking to get a little nooky). While he might respect you, care for you, and truly want to see you, do you really need to get up, shower, and take a cab over to see him—just so you can kiss a few hours earlier? Being so eager to run to see him sends the message that you're willing to accept whatever he's willing to give you. You may think it's worth it in the beginning, but this could set a habit of blurred boundaries in the future.

Real-World Suggestion You deserve a real date. With food. Wait for one.

Bad Potion: Not Taking the Hint

Your fairy-tale take: So he forgot to call you back, missed your birthday party, and left the bar you were supposed to meet at right before you got there. They are all valid reasons for you not seeing him the past couple of weeks. So do you keep e-mailing him to let him know you miss him and are sending him hugs?

Reality: If a suitor is interested in you, he'll make an effort, no matter how shy or busy he might be. That's reality. Even if he were gung ho about you in the beginning, if that's changing, grab your dignity and leave his world without hanging around like a wallflower waiting for him to ask you to dance.

Real-World Suggestion Give your attention to those who give you attention, and your respect to those who respect you.

Bad Potion: Trying to Convince Him to Stay with You

Your fairy-tale take: If only he'd see how great you are compared to other maidens, how much he is throwing away, and how happy he is, he wouldn't want to break up.

Reality: Unfortunately, your view of the relationship is your own. He doesn't appreciate you or value the relationship and wants out because it isn't what he's looking for. Let him go.

Real-World Suggestion You have to respect his desires and not try to guilt him into a role he doesn't want to play (your mate). Besides, if you do "convince" him, there is a very strong chance you are just putting off the inevitable.

Bad Potion: Dating Your Friend's Ex

Your fairy-tale take: Your friend and her guy were college sweethearts who broke up ages ago. You never thought of him in any special way until one thing led to another, and now he's the only lad you can think about. You and your friend have lost touch, and it was a lifetime ago that they dated. What's the big deal?

Reality: There are boundaries and laws governing friendship, and respecting them is what makes you friends. There's a reason Denise Richards and Elizabeth Taylor were vilified in the media after starting a relationship with their best friend's man. No matter what Heather Locklear or Debbie Reynolds might have done, there is a friendship code you just don't crack. If you find yourself interested in dating a friend's ex, be prepared to lose a friend (and the respect of mutual friends). You'll also have constant insecurity issues as you compare relationships and think about what your beau did with your once good friend.

Real-World Suggestion There are a lot of princes out there. Snag one who doesn't carry baggage, which includes someone with whom you have promised loyalty and respect.

Bad Potion: Purposely Making Him Jealous

Your fairy-tale take: A little jealousy keeps him on his toes and reminds him that you are a catch! There's no harm as long as you don't act on it, right?

Reality: There's nothing worse than the sting brought on by the feeling that your relationship is being threatened (which is where jealousy comes from). That is, there's nothing worse except knowing your partner would deliberately put you in that position to "test" your feelings. A loving and respectful relationship is based on and built with trust. While you may feel that chatting up Mr. Soccer Player while your guy orders your favorite drink will only make him want you more, it actually makes him question how you feel about him. No one wants to be in a relationship where they feel unsure.

Real-World Suggestion Playing with someone's emotions is manipulative and cruel. It makes you look insecure and lacking empathy, well, because you are being insecure and lacking empathy.

Bad Potion: Acting like His Girlfriend (When You're Not)

Your fairy-tale take: You really like him, and he mentioned how much he liked jelly beans, so why not pop into his office with a big basket of them one Monday afternoon? You've been seeing one another a couple of weeks, so it's safe to assume you can check "and guest" to your best friend's wedding, right?

Reality: Things might be going great now, but unless you have had "the talk," there's a good chance that he's having a good time with several maidens and is expecting that you are doing the same with other lads. Even if he's seeing only you, if he hasn't asked you to be his girlfriend, introduced you as such, or given you any indication that he would like it to go to a deeper level, DON'T assume that you have the green light to help yourself to his sweatshirt or that you can leave a toothbrush over just because he held your hand a couple of times.

Real-World Suggestion Unlike Cinderella's whirlwind of introduction, stalking, and marriage all in a few days, courtship takes time. Popping it into a pressure cooker by giving yourself a title he has not bestowed upon you is presumptuous and inappropriate. It's like showing up to work before you've been hired.

Royal Revelations:
The Truth About One-Night Stands

"If a woman wants to ruin her chances with a guy, she will try and sleep with him. Some guys might jump at the offer, but the good ones just lose respect for you."
—MARK, TWENTY-SIX, BALTIMORE, MD

"The number one thing a girl can do to kill her chances with me is to sleep with me too soon."
—ALVIN, TWENTY-SEVEN, CRYSTAL LAKE, IL

"You don't want to tell your children you met their mother at a bar and took her home. It might be fun, and you might really like her, but once she does that, the next day you just don't want to see her again."

—HAROLD, THIRTY-ONE, NEW YORK, NY

"Don't sleep with me right away. Sure, slutty girls are great; guys just don't want to date them."

—JEREMY, THIRTY-ONE, WEST CHESTER, OH

"I will respect you tonight but probably not tomorrow."

—STEVE, TWENTY-SEVEN, BOSTON, MA

"There's nothing wrong with random hookups as long as they're treated as such. But don't trash me for not wanting anything more than that. If you expect anything more after a night of screwing after the club, then you're just an idiot."

—MICHAEL, TWENTY-FOUR, NEW BRITAIN, CT

"Don't kid yourself; screwing someone you do not know is not the way to get to spooning."

—STEVE, THIRTY-FIVE, NEW YORK, NY

Chapter 8

The Curse of Verbal Diarrhea

*I*T'S A PHRASE we've all heard but rarely want to admit that it applies to us. Alas, I confess, girls, we all could use a little Beano to aid in our conversational skills every once in a while. How many times have you been enjoying a conversation with a strapping fellow only to find that before you knew it, your foot had snuck up on you and jumped right into your mouth? Suddenly, his smile fades into a look of subtle horror, and you're left wondering how a discussion of your accidental overnight stay in the county loony bin found its way into your conversation about your favorite hotel bars.

As any maiden knows, a small verbal gas spell can be embarrassing, but a bout with verbal diarrhea will leave you more than just embarrassed. It can clog your chances with a prince faster than a paper towel roll shoved down a commode.

What really stinks is that we are such easy targets for this awful curse. I mean, there's no denying that we gals love to gab. Hell, we enjoy it so much that we have created shows dedicated to watching other people do it! Even Cinderella suffered the need to flap her tongue—always singing to herself and telling her stepfamily off under her breath.

While we are writing essays with our words and linking topics with great gusto, our male counterparts are speaking in bullet points—which can make communication a tad complicated for both parties. Here we are, looking to figure out our thesis through discussion, while our poor suitors are usually trying to find enough words to describe their conclusions. When you add in our daily dose of celebrity gossip and discussions about who said what to whom about so-and-so at the grocery store, well, it can leave even the most fantastic guy staring into space, wondering when his brain will stop spinning and you will shut up. This, of course, will have you stewing in no time. Why can't he just pay attention?

Verbal Gas Spells to Avoid

While it's fine to be a chain-talker in the company of females, yammering on about the latest celebrity breakup or what you did in your third-grade talent show can send a prince galloping into the sunset . . . alone. So, even though we've been told silly things like true love knows no secrets or that sharing information about your evil step-aunt's stint in rehab makes you honest and open, the truth is there are some things that should remain secret ingredients in your life's potion—at least until the second date (if not forever!).

Sharing Insecurities About Your Body

I know, I know, you hate your thighs, your bum looks like a dried-up orange peel, and you've taken a liking to empire waists more for the belly than the style. Tell the ladies in your court, but never a suitor or your prince. Whatever lad is dating you (or thinking of dating you) wants to believe they have found a catch. This is more than just a gorgeous maiden with great legs; a catch is someone who feels as good about herself as he feels about her.

For most of us paying the high rents here in reality, confidence changes on a day-by-day, meal-by-meal, and job review–by–job review basis. However, there is a fabulous saying in the theater: what you lack in talent, you make up in style. So while a maiden should never fake an orgasm, a value system, or a hobby, she should fake confidence until she has some. If that's not possible, she should at least keep her insecurities to herself.

Believe it or not, zipping the lips can camouflage the hips. Don't mention your skinny chicken legs, and let him go right on thinking you've got the greatest gams in all of the land. Why? Because sexual attraction is extremely important in the beginning of a relationship. If he's with you and telling you that you're gorgeous, why are you going to try and convince him otherwise? Take every compliment he dishes out and thank him graciously. Don't follow up with any negative comebacks, and suppress your desire to share your thoughts about what you need to do or wish you had. Just a flash of your magical smile will do! Besides, a prince is far more interested in what you think about what is going on in the world than how large you think your booty might be or the fact that you might need a little meat on those bones.

You might bet your favorite pair of Jimmy Choos that he's comparing your bum to the one following Nicole Richie or J. Lo around, but the truth is that most of the time a prince will notice your body "flaws" only when you highlight them in conversation. Telling him how unattractive you think you are will only make him wonder how unattractive you might actually be.

Talking About Your Diet

There are very few things as uninteresting as discussions about your diet. Explaining why you choose to deny yourself something ranks as high on the unsexy scale as a discussion about farming. You might watch your figure, work out two hours a day, and always get your dressing on the side. Or maybe you've chosen to give up meat for specific reasons. That's great if it's how you want to live, but unless you're sitting across from a personal trainer or someone who clearly shares your philosophy, keep it to yourself and try to keep the obsession in check. Ranting and raving about why you refuse to order fries is boring, and coyly mentioning how the burger died will have him asking for the check in no time.

Discussing Female Issues

They don't understand them, and they don't want to.

Sharing the Number of Toads You Have Kissed

So, you've played a bit of leapfrog and kissed your fair share of four-legged creatures in your day. You've dirty danced at more balls with more lads than you'd like to admit to. So don't. What you've done and who you've done is your business, and unless you are being audited, keep that information filed away in your secret box. No matter what a lad says or does, he cares about how many lads came before him (no pun intended). Despite what you might have seen on popular saucy sitcoms or what you've read in your latest issue of *Modern Maiden Magazine*, sleeping with an excessive number of toads and suitors is *not* acceptable in blue-blooded circles. No matter how randy a royal he might be, the number you utter will be too high and will lead to all kinds of judgments, unfair conclusions, and projective imagery on his part. Besides, guys have a terrible double standard when it comes to sexual prowess. They say they don't, but they do.

It may be unfair, but men still believe in the definitions of a lady and a hussy. They will sleep with both, but only one will get his slipper. I know, this sounds chauvinistic, dated—even misogynistic—but the tradition of a prince wanting his princess to be more innocent sexually than he is is not going to die. However, your chances of being more than a fling will if you start blurting out how "liberal" you are. I am not saying not to live your life or to be ashamed of anything you've done, but I am saying that you don't have to tell the whole world about it. That said, if you've done anything that could harm his health or cause him shame and embarrassment, you owe it to him and yourself to speak up. If you went on a tilt in college, be quiet. Contracted a disease or did it on film? Start talking. Also, there is no need to lie about who you are. Just carefully explain to him that you see no reason in sharing things that do not concern your life with him now.

Making Grand Generalizations About a Specific Race, Class, Religion, or Political Affiliation

I should not have to explain why bringing these subjects up on a date is a no-no, but you'd be surprised at the number of suitors who have complained about having a maiden commit one of these conversational faux pas. One suitor excused himself at the end of her sentence by saying, "Yeah, this is definitely not going to work out."

You have no idea who this man is, who his friends are, or what his beliefs might be. On top of that, I would seriously encourage anyone who feels the need to make these kinds of comments to question why they think a racist joke is appropriate or why they are passing judgments on an entire group of people. It's a conversation you should have with yourself, but never with a new suitor.

Dishing the Celebrity Dirt

Who doesn't love a little dish? We gals talk about celebrities as though we know them on a first-name basis. How we love to analyze their lives! In this celebrity-obsessed world, it's hard not to get caught up in who's doing what (and whom) in the ultimate fantasyland gone wrong known as Hollywood. This may seem like a harmless guilty pleasure to you, but to a potential prince this is not only boring but questionable behavior.

When a maiden knows more about a celebrity breakup than she does about what's happening in the Middle East, it shows a serious imbalance of priorities and a lack of passion for her own life. After all, why else would you be so interested in the lives of people you do not know? Now, I know this is not true. I mean, we all love to read about who was seen out on Sunset with whose ex, but guys just don't get the obsession.

We all know that dropping the gossip cold turkey is not an option, so just keep your addiction to yourself. Sweep your *Us Weekly* magazine under your bed as he does his issue of *Saucy Maiden Magazine*. The best way to look like a star is to save the celeb update for girls' night out and let your own life and his life take center stage when you're with him.

Talking About the Ex Factor

We've heard not to do it a thousand times, and yet we've done it a thousand and one. Bringing up the ex is poison for a new relationship. How would you feel if he ranted or raved about a woman in his past all night? Always remember, no matter how much a suitor thinks he wants to know it all, he only wants to know it all until you tell him. As soon as you confess the details, your current beau wishes he could forget them, but he never will. Regardless of whether he was a fantastic suitor or a terrible toad, your ex was not your prince and is gone for a reason. Your new potential royal doesn't need to know that you guys spent the weekend in Vermont or how he once broke your window in a jealous rage. Don't mention your last man unless you're asked about him, and even then keep it light. Talking too much about a former beau tells a prince that you're still battling old emotional demons and worse, that he might have to fight battles based on insecurities and habits that were planted by another man. In addition, every relationship is different according to the dynamic. Thus, it would be unfair to you to allow your new suitor to judge you by your actions in—or reactions to—a relationship that clearly didn't have a happy ending. There's a good chance you've grown since moving on, so allow yourself the chance to put a fresh and new face forward.

Acting as Though He's Your Therapist

Unless she's been locked in a tower, no princess-to-be has ever gotten through life without a few nicks and scratches. But that doesn't mean you need to show him your tender spots just yet. Revealing your battle wounds before he's had a chance to get to know who you are now is a potion for disaster. Whether you went through a heavy party phase after college, you don't speak to your parents, or you wrestled depression, it's best to keep your personal hardships to yourself until he has had a chance to know who you are now.

Most people shy away from things they perceive as too much drama or intensity until there has been a bond formulated. While sharing embarrassing or painful times is a way of establishing intimacy, drowning him in your past sorrows will send him down the river of no return.

Let's be clear. I am in no way suggesting you hide things that could have a potential effect on his health or safety or things that clearly are not in sync with what he is looking for—just those things that have the potential of giving him the wrong idea and might be better understood once he's learned more about you. There's nothing shameful about being on antianxiety medication, but unless he has gotten to know you, he might misinterpret the information and not give the relationship a chance. Just use your common sense. It's one thing to avoid mentioning the time you tried pot in college and another to hide that you were recently arrested for dealing it!

Sharing Negative Stories About Your Friends and Family

Everyone has got some wacky branches hanging off of their family tree. And who doesn't have a friend that could use a lesson in keeping her knickers on? Still, as juicy a story as Lucy's tryst with William and Peter might be, a maiden who speaks ill of her friends or family speaks volumes about her loyalty and respect for the people in her life, or shall we say *a lack thereof.*

There is a wave of discomfort that comes over people when they hear a new friend or a date spill the secrets or highlight the nasty traits of a person in his or her close circle. Telling a date how evil your stepsisters are may seem like a good way to keep the chitchat fresh and funny. However, it will backfire when he starts to wonder if you share things in common with those about whom you speak or if you will be speaking the same way about him one day.

Sharing the personal details of their lives makes you look like a sellout, while highlighting their more unattractive traits makes you guilty by association. Besides, if you want to continue seeing him, he will eventually meet the people you have spoken of and judge them unfairly. It's best to keep the conversation positive and avoid mentioning your best friend's pregnancy scare.

Passing Judgment on His Friends and Family

He might think his best friend is an alcoholic and his mother is overbearing, but offer up your opinion and you'll be sailing solo in no time. He has emotional ties to his drunken bud, and his mother is the apple of his eye, which is why he can say these things about them and still feel as though he's not being disloyal or disrespectful (which is not to say he is right).

You are a different story. He doesn't have an emotional attachment to you. Therefore, any negative comments you make about the people in his life will be met with a defensive and an unpleasant reaction—whether he verbalizes it or not. Also, avoid the whole devil's advocate game. It will only make him feel that you are discounting his feelings by taking an opposing side. Let him speak, make your own judgment, and keep it to yourself. Try moving the conversation to a more neutral topic.

Zip It, Lady! Stop Chatting Aimlessly

We gals chat about everything, don't we? In our vocabulary, silence usually means something is wrong, so we try to fill every inch of dead air with something so as to avoid the deafening sound of silence.

Our suitors are just the opposite; quiet time for them can be as fulfilling and tranquil as a good conversation can be for us. So instead of squeezing every last thought out of your brain, celebrate your differences and try it his way for a change once in a while. Take a walk and hold hands in silence. Chances are the verbal space you provide him will allow him to open up more than he would if you just keep yammering on with brain-numbing information. Maintain a little mystery. Give him a chance to speak and the freedom to enjoy a beautiful moment without a narrator.

The Antidote for Verbal Diarrhea

Here are a few more tips to help keep you on the right track.

~ Talk about where you have traveled and where you would like to travel, and always ask him where he has gone or where he would like to visit.

~ Don't curse or use a lot of slang, even if he does. It makes you sound unintelligent.

~ Live a life that gives you interesting things to talk about! We often fall victim to verbal diarrhea when we run out of things to say.

~ If you like what you do, talk about your job, but don't go overboard. No matter what you do, it's only so interesting to your date. Make sure to ask him about what he does, if he likes it, how long he's been doing it, etc.

~ Tell him where you went to school, and find out where he went. What were some of your favorite things about the town you lived in? What was he like in college?

~ Talk about your current hobbies and interests, and ask him about his.

~ Tell him where you are from, and ask him about where he was born. Did he move a lot? What did he like about it?

~ Think like a journalist: who, what, where, and why. Keep it short, keep it interesting, and always follow it up with a question to show him that you are interested.

~ Think of a few short, funny, nonoffensive stories to share before the date, such as the time you bumped into your favorite actor in a wine store or how you recently went sky-diving, not how you got loaded at a wedding and dove into the fountain. Bad, bad . . . very bad.

Royal Revelations: What Lads Really Think About All That Chatter

"I don't know her life story, and I don't want to know it unless I have made her my girlfriend."

—TED, TWENTY-SIX, VILLANOVA, PA

"Women who go on and on about their life scare me."

—THAD, THIRTY-TWO, EAU CLAIRE, WI

"I have three words for women who find they are talking too much on a date: 'Stop. Look. Listen!'"

—NATIO, TWENTY-THREE, NEW YORK, NY

"Don't talk about your job like it's the most important thing in your life. If you are curing cancer, great, talk on, but if you are the accounts payable person for Smart and Final, chances are a little goes a long way."

—MARTY, THIRTY, LOS ANGELES, CA

"I used to actually like some of your friends, you know. But whenever they are not around you talk about them like they are a stampeding pack of wild huffalumps. Are you really surprised then that I have nothing good to say about them? You yell at me when I say something bad about them, but all I ever hear is how Candice has all this cottage cheese on her ass, or how Sandra has the worst herpes sore on her lip, or how Gina dogged her boyfriend out for some new guy. And to top it off, anytime you have a problem with me, the first thing out of your mouth is Candice thinks you have insecurity issues. Gina says you should read sex tips for men. So please tell why I have to be nice to your friends. You hate them, and now I hate them too."

—JUSTIN, THIRTY, LOS ANGELES, CA

"Please don't talk about ex-boyfriends or anything indicating you used to be a slut. Sluts are OK to hook up with but not to date. And no one cares about the guy you used to date before."

—TOM, THIRTY-SIX, BRYN MAWR, PA

"Women who ramble on are such a turnoff. I like listening to other people, but I, much like most people, also like *talking* about things that interest me. Extreme long-windedness turns into boredom very quickly. Also, it causes me to tune her out so I can think about something that will keep me awake."

—STEVE, THIRTY-FIVE, NEWPORT, RI

Chapter 9

---•---

Guaranteed Ways
to Send Him Far, Far Away

*L*OOK AT HOW far you have come since we started! I am so happy for you! You have taken the time to date and get to know yourself and really listened to your emotional intuition. You know what it's like to walk barefoot, and you've tried on a few slippers and moved on when you realized they didn't fit your foot, lifestyle, or personality.

You didn't rush things or place yourself in some kind of dating race, which is why you are thrilled to be seeing the new, fantastic suitor you met while out living your life. This lad is truly something special and is the reason you've been floating from moment to moment.

You have gotten through your first eight weeks of dating, you've made it through your first fight unscathed, and he's even given you a drawer at the castle. Things are running smoothly, and you've both decided to make this an exclusive situation. I know you are feeling more confident about the whole situation, and he's even mentioned taking you home to meet the queen. (OK, so he was a little tipsy.)

In fact, things are moving along *so well*, you've started to believe that you're in the clear and that this whole slipper thing is a done deal. Hold it right there, Miss Comfort—else you wish to find yourself with a nasty little rock in your shoe!

Six Months in Purgatory

What is it? How did you get there? How does one avoid falling into the pits of dating hell? "Six months in purgatory" is exactly what it implies—six months in an uncertain time in which you lie somewhere between the status of "a cool girl I'm seeing" and "I'm taking you home to Mom."

Sure, your suitor might really like spooning you on Sunday afternoons and think you're supersexy when you're making coffee runs in his gym shorts, but don't let that fool you. You are still totally disposable with little discomfort in his eyes. Getting too cozy in purgatory will have him on his horse faster than you can dash to a Barney's sale. So, before you start criticizing his friends, trying to change his style, or nagging him to come over when he's told you he wants to relax at home, take a look at the things that are guaranteed to send him far, far away.

Send Him Galloping: By Trying to Mold Him

You think he would be great if only he'd change his style, dump his loser best friend, or kick the poker obsession. Stop it right there! Trying to change a lad is exhausting, disappointing, and frustrating—and that's just for him! Your suitor has been the person he is most of his life, and he's perfectly fine with it or he would change it himself. Like you, he's a culmination of experiences, memories, preferences, and dislikes, and there's a good chance that he and the people in his life enjoy who that person is. He was doing just fine until now and even garnered your interest along the way! What in the world makes you think he is OK with you coming in and attempting to rearrange his personality?

Why We Do It

A lot of maidens look at their guys as fixer-uppers, when in reality, no matter how you dress him or what you force him to do with you on a Sunday afternoon, he's still the guy who loves wearing wrinkled T-shirts, playing Xbox, and lounging around in his PJs all weekend. He's just going to be a lot more resentful. You can paint a house any way you'd like, but the basic foundation and structure will remain the same.

Putting the Slipper on the Other Foot

So, if he has made it clear that his living in sweats and hating the opera were all part of the deal when you two met, don't try and dress him in Versace and introduce him to Maria Callas via the local opera house. A suitor may very well be your prince, but it might end your chances at the crown if he feels that you are trying to mold him into something he's not. Sure, he might endure a romantic comedy once in a while to appease you, but don't ever expect him to choose a Madonna concert with you over a night with the guys.

Real-World Suggestion How would you feel if he told you how to dress, told you how to cut your hair, or berated you for not liking football? Trying to change him suggests that you find something embarrassing or wrong with the person he is, which will only make him question whether or not you are the right maiden for him. In fact, if you are trying to make him over, you might want to question it yourself.

Send Him Galloping: By Trying to Control Him

This is a huge mistake we maidens make once we get into a relationship with a suitor. How many times have you watched one of your male friends take on a new girlfriend only to never hear from him again? How about watching your brother morph into a spineless sap who now dresses in an entirely new way because his new wife likes him better in Polo? What is so interesting is that we can all sit around and complain about his new gal with ease and somehow not realize that the friends of our own guy are saying the same things about us!

Why We Do It

Look, ladies, just because a suitor takes your feelings into consideration doesn't mean your feelings should be the only ones that matter or that they trump the feelings of his friends or his own in any way. Throwing tantrums over boys' night, forcing him to come to your place and cook dinner for the fifth time in a week, or causing a fight over his desire to spend the weekend apart is enough to make any lad want to stay a confirmed bachelor.

Putting the Slipper on the Other Foot

It's so interesting how we want to force these guys to have brunch with us or hold our bags as we try on the umpteenth sundress, but dare they want to grab a beer with coworkers after work, we throw a fit!

Your suitor is his own person with his own feelings and opinions and his own likes and dislikes. Let him make his own decisions and do his own thing, and pay attention to his choices, actions, and reactions. In doing so you will have not only a better understanding of him as a person but also a higher likelihood of knowing whether or not he is your prince.

Real-World Suggestion How would you like it if he freaked out about your decision to have a weekend lunch with your girlfriends or told you what to wear? Would you like to follow him from one sports store to another, holding his bags? You are not his mother or his warden—remember that. Besides, what are you afraid of? There is a good chance your wanting to control him and the situation stems from an insecurity you have. Focus your attention on controlling that.

Send Him Galloping: By Letting Jealousy Rear Its Ugly Head

Now, no one is saying not to put the smackdown on the Victoria's Secret model type who's draped on your man like butter on popcorn. However, if your suitor is a good-looking man who has always been faithful and you are putting him on lockdown, it's time to uncuff him.

Being jealous is like throwing a noose around the neck of the relationship, which can cause both partners to choke and suffocate every time he tries to move through his life independently.

Why We Do It
You don't need a Ph.D. to know that jealousy is based on insecurity, and insecurity can act like a devil on your shoulder.

It can motivate you to say and do things that come across as downright evil in the eyes of a potential prince.

The issue when dealing with situations that make your stomach twist and twirl is whether your feelings and reactions are based on something significant or on your own made-up worries about what might happen. There is no denying that sometimes there is cause for a jealous reaction, but most of the time—with a good guy—there isn't.

Putting the Slipper on the Other Foot

If you're feeling threatened, ask yourself if your feelings are truly based on his actions or if they're based on unfounded fears. Are you projecting your insecurities onto him? Is he paying for the evil deeds done by a slimy ex? Or is he disrespecting the agreement you both made about being exclusive and purposely playing with your emotions? If this is the case, you've nabbed a toad. Dump him.

Here is what one suitor had to say about the common green-eyed monster: "Jealousy is a huge turnoff for men. Have you ever had to deal with a superjealous boyfriend? It's just as annoying on the other side of the fence." The bottom line is that we're all individual people, and we have to trust one another to honor the commitments we have made while not hindering one another's rights to be their own person.

Real-World Suggestion Regardless of the reasons, swimming in a swamp of frustration and worry while being bitten by this ugly green-eyed monster is no way to go through a relationship. If you're worrying about his future actions or your interpretation of the actions of others (such as his best girlfriends), you're going to have to seek some kind of help. You've got to get to the source of your anxiety because this is not about him. Taking him down with you as you continuously throw yourself into the murky water of doubt will grow tiresome fast. He might save you a couple of times, but soon he will tire of the emotional currents beneath the water and let you drown.

Send Him Galloping: By Letting Yourself Go

I may take a lot of heat for this, but I am willing to be the bearer of controversial news to help out my fellow maidens. It may sound a bit trite, but the fact is, attraction matters in a relationship. It matters a lot. In fact, attraction is what makes a sexual relationship different from a friendship. When you stop taking care of yourself or making an effort, it will inevitably take a toll on you, on your partner, and on the relationship as a whole.

No one is saying you have to look like a supermodel to keep a man's interest or that if, God forbid, a life event occurs that has an effect on your looks he will leave you. (That's a toad with no empathy.) But making the choice to *not* comb your hair, wear comfortable-yet-flattering clothing, and make an effort to remain healthy and attractive screams that you just don't care anymore. Accurate or not, it sends the message to your mate that screams, "Now that I have you, turning you on is a nonissue." He may not leave you, but he's sure to resent you, and he'll definitely find you less appealing!

Why We Do It

Taking care of yourself is an outward sign of what's going on inside. Though we have been taught to vilify wanting to look good and call it vanity, there is absolutely nothing wrong with wanting to look attractive. This does not mean you need to dress like a hussy or fulfill his Carmen Electra fantasies by trying to be something you are not; it simply means putting your own best foot forward. Making this effort can enhance your relationship in more ways than one.

As I said, for most of us, the difference between romantic and platonic love is physical attraction and sexual chemistry. These two components are not superficialities but passionate and exciting parts of life! I am not discounting the importance of intimacy, trust, mutual respect, and encouragement, but you can have all of these things with your closest friends. Think about it, gals. We don't go gaga over Clooney and Pitt because they are funny! Milton Berle was a funny guy, but he hardly caused the same reaction as Paul Newman.

Unfortunately, in the real world, we gals have been taught to ignore the sexual and desirous parts of ourselves. We're told that "good girls" don't enjoy sex, or that it's wrong to yearn for a man just because he's sexy. Like Cinderella's crap about perfect love, this is total baloney! There is nothing wrong with being attracted to someone or placing value on what a person looks like. It shouldn't be the only thing that motivates you when seeking a mate, but it shouldn't be something of no value either! You can have wonderful bonds and emotional attachments to your closest male friends, but, unless you're attracted to them, they will never be the one you are dying to dance with and kiss at the ball.

Putting the Slipper on the Other Foot

This is why our suitors have an inherent fear of their mates "giving up" once they are committed to them. They were not taught to ignore their sexuality, and they are visual creatures, which means that attraction plays a key role in their relationships (not sexual encounters, but relationships). When you meet a suitor, he's interested in you based on who you are and what you look like, just as you are. He makes a commitment to the person you are at that point in your life, and he is attracted to you. He's signing up for something that both turns him on and makes him happy.

Ever find yourself eyeing the cute guy on the street that reminds you of your prince of a few years ago? Wish your guy would get a haircut and make the small efforts to look and smell good as he did when you first met? You are doing the same thing he's doing.

Real-World Suggestion Letting yourself go by no longer taking the time to try and look your best or maintain yourself can (and will) have an effect on his attraction to you. It can also cause resentment when he starts to wonder why you don't care enough about him to take the time and try to look nice for him. This doesn't make him a bad guy; it makes him human. A more important question is what in the world is going on that you don't want to look and feel good for yourself?

Send Him Galloping: By Placing a Wedge Between Him and His Friends

You love your guy but hate his friends. It's a story as old as Cinderella's. Be warned, ladies, the ending will be far from happy if you try and pry him away from bonds that meant as much to him as you do long before you came into his life.

Why We Do It

Now, we all know his former fraternity brothers are trolls, but whether or not he spends Sunday afternoons with them is not our decision to make. We maidens tend to fear that our mate will be influenced by his friends' bad behavior or that his buddies are immature and unfocused. If he's that weak-minded, do you really want to be with him?

Putting the Slipper on the Other Foot

Here's the reality: all lads like to goof off and act thirteen every once in a while, and the best place for them to do this is with their pals. They want to let loose and not have to be on their best behavior, excusing their belches or denying the fact that the new *Playboy* has a great pictorial. Just like we like to shop, talk, and get our pedicures, our suitors have their own routines they like to enjoy. This doesn't mean that Man Slut Steve is going to put the cheating voodoo on your guy, but he will most likely get him out drinking while he searches for his next conquest, and as long as your suitor maintains his commitment to you, that is OK.

Think about your girlfriends that annoy your guy. How many times have you told him to "be nice" to your mother? Respecting your right to make your own decisions about your time and who you spend it with is something that shows you he cares about you and respects you. As long as the vows and commitments you make to one another are being respected, there's no reason to fear boys' night out.

Real-World Suggestion When we get into relationships with our partners, we inevitably get into relationships with their friends and family—two groups that are made up of individual people and personalities. We probably won't like them all, but this doesn't mean we should expect our mates to share our feelings or abide by our new rules not to be around so-and-so. That's not fair. We don't own them. Unless these people are disrespecting you or your mate is placing a higher value on drinks with the boys than your birthday, it's best to smile and put petty differences aside; otherwise you're likely to come across as a wicked, witchy girlfriend.

Send Him Galloping: By Stalking Him

There is a very special place reserved in the minds of suitors for stalkers. They've all had one, and they've all reduced her to bar fodder. She's become a war story for new girlfriends and pals who are complaining about the current chick who showed up unannounced last weekend.

Why We Do It

Maidens often convince themselves and one another that situations are more intense than they are and will support and even encourage erratic and crazy behavior. We assume lads are up to no good and act accordingly.

Putting the Slipper on the Other Foot

Imagine some guy you barely knew or one you weren't interested in showing up randomly, putting you on the spot, or following your every move. It's creepy, and you owe yourself and your reputation more than being someone suitors try and avoid.

Real-World Suggestion The fact is, driving past his place to see if he's home when he said he needed to study isn't normal, and it shows zero trust. Worse, if he sees you, he'll end things because he'll think you're an insecure psycho. Calling him from blocked numbers and hanging up is immature, and stopping by work when he hasn't returned your call *is* stalking!

Send Him Galloping: By Cheating on Him

Cheating on someone says that you are not only completely selfish and unable to maintain any kind of self-control but also that you care very little about the person you're with. You're risking his health and happiness and taking his love for granted.

Why We Do It

You'd think this was a no-brainer, but more and more maidens are playing the field and making "errors in judgment" while in relationships with good guys. There is a huge misconception that men are more prone to cheating than we are.

Putting the Slipper on the Other Foot

How would you feel if someone you loved, trusted, and made a commitment to threw all of that away for one night of pleasure? Worse, think about them sneaking back to you and putting their lips, hands, and body on top of yours. Yuck.

Real-World Suggestion There is a moment when you decide you want to cheat, and in that moment you can break up with the person who is giving you all of his trust. You might be seen as a heartless witch, but at least you are respecting him enough to be honest and not lying and betraying him. You deserve to be happy in life but not at the expense of someone else's trust and happiness.

Send Him Galloping: By Using Him

Whether you are rocking out in great seats at concerts, laughing over great dinners in the best restaurants, or lying in the sand by his beach house, you are always having such a great time. The question is, are you dating him or in it for his awesome hookups? Where would you be if he started taking you to pubs and diners?

Why We Do It

He's a really great guy and you like him a lot. You're just not sure he's the one for you. I mean, he's kind of cute, and you have a lot of fun together, but you don't feel the chemistry lighting sparks. You'd love to have a talk with him about it, but the fact that you have such a great time together makes it really hard to be up front. How can you make an objective decision about him when he's buying you Prada, sending you flowers, and taking you to U2?

Putting the Slipper on the Other Foot

A lad who pretends to like you and just wants sex is a toad, and one who takes you out as arm candy is a superficial loser. What are your actions saying about you? Kanye West and Ray Charles would know.

Real-World Suggestion A user is a loser, and you deserve to hold yourself up to higher standards. Stand on your own two feet, buy your own damn concert tickets, and send yourself an orchid! Being an independent woman allows you total control and the confidence to pick and choose who you spend time with on a romantic level. You can even keep this great guy as a friend and set him up with your coworker who would look so cute with him. Best of all, he will respect you and your totally intact reputation.

Send Him Galloping: By Invading His Privacy

He's been coming home late a lot lately, and you wonder what really happened on that recent trip to Vegas. Curiosity is killing you, which is why when he leaves his e-mail open you are more than eager to click out the truth.

Why We Do It

Going through someone's e-mail is like reading their diary and fishing through their belongings for clues. It's a violation of their basic human right to privacy. If he finds out you are in his business, you can be sure you will be put on probation or fired from his life. If he never finds out that you are snooping, you can be sure he will feel the cold air of lack of trust.

Putting the Slipper on the Other Foot

Imagine how it would feel to come home and see your underwear drawer opened and rummaged through or your diary wide open? Just because you hide the evidence doesn't mean you're not robbing him of his rights.

Your actions are bound to have an effect on your relationship. How could they not? You clearly don't trust the person you are with, and the fact that you're willing to sneak around and betray him signifies a severe lack of respect for your partner that will surely transcend into other aspects of your relationship.

Real-World Suggestion If you don't trust him, break up with him, but don't be a deceitful sneak. You're better than that.

Ways to Get Him to Stay for the Sunrise

OK, now that we know how to send him on his way, let's talk about the things every maiden can do to make him want to share waffles in the morning. It's a silly misconception that men need less nurturing and appreciation than we do. Here are several ways to keep him coming back for more.

Pay Attention to Him!

Cinderella had a habit of sharing every last detail of her day with her prince, rarely stopping to catch her breath, let alone ask him about his day.

Everyone wants to feel that his or her life matters, and he's no different. It's a natural human desire to know that one's thoughts, feelings, and accomplishments are noted by someone else. This is why taking the time to really listen to a suitor—to ask him how his day was or his opinion on something—can go a long way. Many of us get so caught up in our daily lives and thoughts that we overlook those of the people who are closest to us. You don't need to interrogate him or get mad if he doesn't feel like chatting, but do check in and try and remember little things he says about his past, his dreams, etc.

Compliment Him!

Cinderella was old-school and left it up to her prince to court and compliment her. Her prince felt as though he was always doting on her twenty-four–seven with no acknowledgment of his own positive traits. When one of the maidens in Cindy's court told the prince how much she admired him, his chest puffed out and a huge smile ran across his face. Cinderella immediately accused the prince of flirting, not realizing she was forgetting to water his spirit.

How great is it when a sexy suitor tells you that you look beautiful, that he is stunned by your intelligence, or that he loves your sense of humor? Sincere compliments are small, priceless gifts that lift spirits and connect us. If he looks nice, tell him! If you find his guitar strumming has gotten better, let him know. Appreciation, respect, and acknowledgment are the best resentment repellants.

Make Him Laugh!

Cinderella never developed her sense of humor and took everything quite personally. She believed in being proper over being lighthearted, which made her seem uptight and boring to her prince.

You don't have to be Lucille Ball, but please, lighten up! Laughing is naturally very sexy; your body is relaxed and smiling is contagious. Being serious and being taken seriously are two very different things that are commonly interlinked by us. Loosen up, and he'll open up.

Respect His Opinion!

Cinderella constantly battled her prince and had a nasty habit of devaluing his opinions, which led to intense fights and serious resentment.

Don't forget that your suitor is a human being, and each person perceives the world in a very different way. You don't have to agree with him or even understand his thought process on certain things, but that does not mean you have a right to devalue his opinion. Let him know you disagree, but don't ever make it personal.

Give Him Space When He Needs It!

Cinderella wanted to spend every last moment with her prince and often felt rejected and dejected when he would "zone out."

Allow your suitor to be alone and think, without crowding him or expecting him to share his feelings twenty-four–seven. Our suitors process information differently from the way we do. They see talking about their problems as a sign of weakness in that they feel talking with someone about their issues is the same as asking for advice. This is why every time you talk with him about problems he offers you solutions (leaving you wanting to toss him off of your own horse!). It's a story as old as Cinderella's: gals want to talk about their feelings about the problem, and men want to fix it.

Romance Him!

Cinderella taught us that it's up to a prince to court us, kiss us, save us, and make us feel like princesses.

He may not need candles and roses, but it's a fallacy that lads don't enjoy and desire romance. We often nag at our suitors that they aren't romantic by the standards set by both Cindy and Hollywood. The thing is, we gripe and snipe and then dismiss his desires as unimportant, annoying, or offensive. Maybe romantic to him is going to a game, noshing on hot dogs, and swigging beers. Maybe he thinks staying home and cuddling on the couch is more romantic than spending a fortune at a restaurant. Ask him what he finds romantic, and make the effort. Chances are he'll do the same for you.

Avoid Spouting Clichés About Men!

Every time Cinderella got together with her court, her prince would hear them go on and on about how dumb, silly, or ridiculous lads were. She thought it was funny. He found it annoying and offensive.

There's a huge double standard when it comes to voicing opinions about the opposite sex. Calling men pigs or pathetic and using other degrading terms and phrases are common ways of addressing our opposite gender. We giggle and throw out verbal assaults with wild abandon, and yet we don't seem to think about the effect our words might have on our suitors. Assuming all lads can't be trusted with common tasks or to honor their commitment makes you look like an insensitive and misinformed chick with no empathy. Just as you're not like every other maiden in the land, each suitor is an individual, and all individuals deserve respect.

A Little Reminder

Honing your empathy, sympathy, and self-respect are the three best ways to avoid crossing over someone else's boundaries. Also, make sure that yours are being honored as well. Every guy and gal who enter into a relationship are choosing to share their life and experiences with someone, but that doesn't mean they need to give up their rights or likes or change what is at their core.

Respect the individuality, privacy, opinions, and desires of your prince, just as you're hoping he will respect yours. If he's the right man for you, he will reciprocate, and you'll both trot off into the sunset smiling.

Chapter 10

The Lads Holding You Back and the Toads Who Have to Go

K GALS, GRAB those proverbial brooms and get a bunch of trash bags because we're about to toss out the lads and toads who are cluttering your heart and making it impossible for your prince to move in! It's time to do a little spring cleaning in the romance department!

By this chapter, I am hoping that you have started to gain a better understanding of what it means to be in the right romantic situation and how better to obtain it. I'm hoping that you place a higher value on your commitment and who you give it to and truly accept that you deserve to be in a healthy, respectful relationship that makes you happy (and so do your suitors and princes). I think by now we all understand that there's no such thing as a perfect relationship or mate, and this is OK because in the real world, nothing is pristine, organized, and lovely all of the time. We all know that Cinderella lied and that perfection is great in theory but impossible in application. By reading the chapters before this one, I'm hoping that you have finally learned to accept that *compromise* isn't a bad word. It's an essential aspect of the balance and harmony of life—not only in your romantic relationships but in all of your relationships with people (and even in the relationship you have with yourself).

Now, with all of this self-discovery and accountability, you might have looked over an important aspect of dating, which is protecting yourself from the wrong suitors. That's right, ladies, it ain't always your fault. There are lads out there who are just bad, and nothing you say or do is going to change them, so don't even waste your time.

While you might have learned that compromising is the key to happiness, it is only going to unlock the door to romantic fulfillment as long as you're not compromising in the areas involving your value system, happiness, sense of self-worth, or emotional, physical, or mental well-being and freedom. You simply cannot get to your happy ending by wasting your time on lads who are emotionally unavailable to you or have severe emotional issues.

The Lads Who Are Holding You Back— Who Are They, Really?

There is a difference between a lad who has issues and a toad who is using you, but the end result is the same; stay with either and you are bound to get stuck in a rut and wind up with a cracked or shattered heart. You'll remain barefoot and bitter as your romantic life slowly passes you by. A lad you need to cut loose is not a toad but a suitor with too many issues to ever be in a healthy relationship. These issues have nothing to do with you, but that won't stop you from trying to take them on, one by one, exhausting yourself and leaving you tired and troubled at the end of the long and draining days. Whether he's irresponsible, self-centered, or attached to his mother's bosom, you will need to show him the door before you are ever greeted by a prince with a slipper that will properly fit your foot.

Many maidens have dated that one suitor who made them question whether or not he was looking for a prince of his own to snag. Now, this lad is not bad for being gay; he's bad for not being honest about his situation and choosing to lead you into believing you will ever have a meaningful, long-term, romantic relationship with him. The fact is, by keeping his real feelings or confusions inside, he's being utterly irresponsible with your heart. If he is using you to hide his true self, he's being cruel. See the descriptions that follow to find out if your lad is in the closet or is one of the others holding you back.

The Lad Who's in the Closet

HIS STYLE: Vintage jeans, sleek button-downs, maroon leather jacket, great accessories, and hot sunglasses. He dresses to impress daily—you love his style!

WHAT YOU'LL FIND IN HIS MEDICINE CABINET: He has the best products! Bronzers, under-eye cream, and masks. You love sleeping over because playing in his bathroom is the BEST way to start your day. His shampoos make your hair smell phenomenal.

OCCUPATION: These guys can do everything well—and with flair.

WHERE YOU'LL MEET HIM: Melrose Avenue, Soho, Crate and Barrel on the weekends, fabulous brunch places, and the hottest clubs—in VIP, of course. He rocks the scene.

HIS SIGNATURE PHRASES: "This dress is sick! Try it on!" "Have you ever thought of getting highlights, just at the crown?" "I love musicals!"

WHY HE'S BAD FOR YOU: He's not a toad; he's great and you love him. How could you not? He's a blast! The thing is, you never really feel that "close" when you both crawl into his thousand-thread-count sheets. Let me tell you why. You don't have a penis. You never will. It's going to crush you, but you have to end it. However, stay friends. He's great for image consulting.

The Rich Prick Lad

HIS STYLE: He thinks he's a Kennedy but voted for Bush. Perfectly pressed tailored suits, French cuffs—if it's top of the line, he owns it. When you give him a tie from Banana Republic, he gives you a condescending smile and gently reminds you that he only wears ones from Pink. This is the guy who gives to charity and tells you about it while writing the check.

WHAT YOU'LL FIND IN HIS MEDICINE CABINET: Moisturizer, Viagra (no matter what his age), shaving brush, and plated razor.

OCCUPATION: Banker, heir, real estate mogul, Daddy's boy, president of the boy's club and the yacht club (though he hates the water).

WHERE YOU'LL MEET HIM: Martini bars, Cape Cod, Nantucket, East Hampton, Miami, and above 34th Street in Manhattan.

HIS SIGNATURE PHRASES: "You did 'camp' in the summer; I did the Cape." "I only drink vintage."

WHY HE'S BAD FOR YOU: No matter how much you try to please him, he'll always be one step ahead of you. You'll never be good enough because he is the one setting the standards—and they are so expensive you can't afford to even think about reaching them. This guy gets off on living out his "Dynasty" dreams, and unless you share the same background or bank

True Story

He was quite the catch with his tailored suits, attention to detail, perfectly decorated summer home, and snazzy shoe collection. He always had a table at the hottest restaurants and drank martinis the old-fashioned way—in a tumbler "just like Cary Grant," he said. I likened him to a modern fifties matinee idol and was all about him until the one night he pulled me into his bedroom at a party and scolded me for wearing two varying shades of brown by way of my belt and shoes.

It was at that moment I had the flashbacks:

- The bronzer in his medicine cabinet!
- The day dates of shopping around town!
- The one night he mentioned the size of his friend's penis while we were in bed!
- The time he told me he wouldn't go out with me and my friends to the Abby because he "only went to the gay clubs in New York."

Then, of course, there was also the most incriminating piece of evidence to date: his vintage Louis Vuitton bag. It finally occurred to me. My guy was no Cary Grant! He was Rock Hudson! He was not my sensitive, stylish suitor! He was a lad in the closet, using me to hide his secret from the world.

I immediately questioned him about his extreme metrosexuality, and he just laughed. "Ha! Ha!" he said. But I ask you, was it a coincidence he dumped me ten days later? I think not.

The truth is, breaking up with this suitor broke both my heart and my bank account. I had to start buying all of the fantastic facial creams I used to sneak in his bathroom, and drinks at the hottest clubs aren't cheap!

Oh, and by the way, Mr. Pseudo Gay, I know you didn't "lose" my eyelash curler.

account, you're always going to be at the mercy of his money and his inflated ego. Only a fool would waste her precious time running around like a monkey trying to please this self-centered snot. Move on, or don't complain when he does—and my goodness, lady, stop buying things you can't afford just to keep up. Otherwise you'll wind up single *and* broke!

The Lad Having a Midlife Crisis (AKA Mr. Tomorrow)

HIS STYLE: Khakis, Polo shirts, and baseball hats on the weekends; slick suits at the office. There might be a ponytail or hair plugs involved.

WHAT YOU'LL FIND IN HIS MEDICINE CABINET: Overscented grooming products, facial creams, condoms, and maybe a few items left over from his soon-to-be-ex-wife.

OCCUPATION: He could have been an agent, producer, entertainment executive, lawyer, broker, plastic surgeon, or entrepreneur. Now he is a wine connoisseur.

WHERE YOU'LL MEET HIM: Riding around on his Harley or in his new two-seater. Drinking Scotch at hotel bars or occasionally out with his son and his son's girlfriends at the hottest nightspots. Taking out his boat on the weekends. Sometimes you'll be invited; other times, you won't.

HIS SIGNATURE PHRASES: "I feel like I am twenty years old in my heart!" "Look, I am not really in the mood to discuss this right now; let's talk about it tomorrow." "I'll be out of town on business for a couple of weeks, but I'll call you as soon as I return home." "Can't we just have some fun tonight without the heavy stuff? Let's enjoy what we have."

WHY HE'S BAD FOR YOU: This lad is living in the past he never had because he didn't have the means. He can't even commit to being middle-aged, and you're expecting him to "have the talk" with you? The only thing he's going to be popping is your hopes for a commitment and maybe some Möet on his sailboat. Get over it. He's interested in "living for now" because he fears death, and before he gets there he is hoping that a few sets of perky breasts will make him feel alive. He's stringing you along, and you're following like a no-brainer. Wise up and ditch this procrastinator because "tomorrow" isn't "only a day away."

The Lad Who's a Slacker

HIS STYLE: Jeans, vintage Ts daily. Often, the same ones . . .

WHAT YOU'LL FIND IN HIS MEDICINE CABINET: A disgusting mess. His products are expired, his toothpaste cap is hard and gooey, and his Gold Bond powder is nearly empty. Still, it was nice that his parents put a bathroom in the basement for him like that.

OCCUPATION: Actor, writer, musician, perpetual student, or "student of life."

WHERE YOU'LL MEET HIM: Coffee shops, house parties, Irish pubs, walking around aimlessly in your apartment, eating all of your food.

HIS SIGNATURE PHRASES: "I am going through a phase right now. I need to find me." "I am not about to sell out and work for the man." "Can I borrow five bucks?"

WHY HE'S BAD FOR YOU: Unless he's bringing in enough to support his lazy bum (while still being able to buy you a taco once in a while), he's not anything but a bum. It's nice to be artistic, but when his dreams become a nightmare for you, it's time to move on—especially if he's borrowing money. If you're asking yourself, "Will he ever get it together?" let me answer you. NO!

The Lad Who's Still Breast-Feeding

HIS STYLE: This guy could be in either Pink button-downs or Gap T-shirts. No matter which style he's sporting, you can count on him having messy hair, dark denim, and a sleek designer wallet all bought on Mama's card.

WHAT YOU'LL FIND IN HIS MEDICINE CABINET: Cold remedies, the Clinique face wash system, Visine, and everything else his mom brought over during her latest visit.

OCCUPATION: Doctor, lawyer, banker, professor—Mama didn't raise no deadbeat!

WHERE YOU'LL MEET HIM: Running errands, brunch with Mom, Saks Fifth Avenue, "Bloomies."

HIS SIGNATURE PHRASES: "I was raised by my mother; I know how to treat a woman." "I know you really want to take the job in Milan, but Mom thinks it's best we stay in Trenton!" "Don't worry about dinner tonight, it's on Mom; she gave me her card."

WHY HE'S BAD FOR YOU: Mama's boys are sweet, kind, thoughtful, and totally whipped. Mom is not about to let Junior lose focus—let alone lose it with the likes of you. To paraphrase the late Princess Diana, there will be three of you in the relationship; are you ready to share your secrets, life, and feelings with her every week? No? That's OK, you won't have to; he will when he drives home for his weekly dinner. Do you really want to spend your life competing with her over holidays and child rearing and having to suffer through her approval and disapproval processes? Find someone without the umbilical cord.

The Lad Who Doesn't Know What He Wants

HIS STYLE: One day he's sporting a suit and polished shoes, and the next he's a sports fanatic who wears only his Adidas flip-flops. He can't commit to one particular style.

WHAT YOU'LL FIND IN HIS MEDICINE CABINET: Tylenol and Advil, hairspray and gel, moustache comb and shaving kit.

OCCUPATION: He works in real estate but thinks he might go back to school to become a doctor; he always did like medicine. Or maybe he'll become a soccer coach. He loves soccer!

WHERE YOU'LL MEET HIM: This man is everywhere!

HIS SIGNATURE PHRASES: "I love rice and beans!" . . . two days later, "I don't eat carbs; I am on Atkins." "I really like you, but I have no idea where I am right now." . . . two days later, "I want to get married."

WHY HE'S BAD FOR YOU: This guy is too busy trying to figure out who he is and what he wants in his life to ever decide to commit to you. Even if you can get him to commit, you have no idea who he will wind up being or how long it will take for him to change his mind again!

The Lad Who Is Not Over His Ex

HIS STYLE: He looks like a normal enough guy—until you realize his ex bought his wardrobe.

WHAT YOU'LL FIND IN HIS MEDICINE CABINET: Her old pink razor and a half-empty bottle of hair serum that smells like peaches.

OCCUPATION: He went and took his GMAT after she left him for a banker. Now he works at Goldman.

WHERE YOU'LL MEET HIM: At the restaurant they used to go to, at the bar where they met, and near her place of work hoping to bump into her.

HIS SIGNATURE PHRASE: "My ex used to . . ."

WHY HE'S BAD FOR YOU: He's missing her and dating you, which means you're a substitute. There is a good chance that if she ever changes her mind you are out, and if she doesn't you are being compared to her constantly. Let him go until he lets her go.

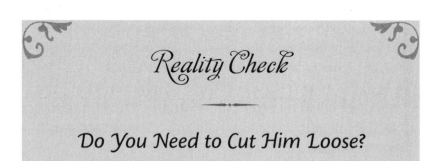

Reality Check

Do You Need to Cut Him Loose?

We have been dating for three months:
A. I know where I stand and how he feels about me.
B. I know he cares for me but is not yet ready to commit.
C. I know he likes pinot noir.

His ex:

A. Was a nice person, but things just didn't work out.

B. Still calls on his birthday; they are friendly.

C. Was a witch who screwed him over, which is why he puts pins in the picture he has by his bed—"for closure."

He makes you feel:

A. Confident, beautiful, and appreciated.

B. A little uneasy, but happy most of the time.

C. Disposable.

His mother:

A. Calls him to remind him to call his father for Father's Day.

B. Calls him to remind him to floss.

C. Has a key to his place.

When it comes to his job:

A. It's all about work when he's there and play when he isn't.

B. He's very committed to the lifestyle it offers him, so he works late a lot.

C. He doesn't really believe in working in the "conventional sense."

His guy friends:

A. Are a solid group who love to get together for poker and drinks.

B. Are his second family, and a bachelor party is in solid competition with your anniversary.

C. Have tickle fights.

Your Answers

Mostly As: He's a solid suitor who could very well be your prince!

Mostly Bs: He might be a suitor, but you will need to think long and hard about what you want out of life and whether you can deal with being second banana to his job, mother, ex, or friends.

Mostly Cs: Snip the strings and let him go so you can find a suitor who will not string you along!

The Toads Who Have Got to Go— How to Recognize a Reptile

We've all heard the old cliché that warns us, "You've got to kiss a lot of toads before you meet your prince." They also used to think the world was flat. Need I say more? This is just another lie, weaved and perpetuated by some chick unable to face the fact that she has willingly put up with bad behavior in order to have someone in her life. Fortunately for you, we've uncovered the truth, and it's very simple. While we might be tricked by a deceptive reptile or charmed by a wart-covered tongue, there is no rule that says you have to pay your dues with scumbags to meet a good guy. Oh, and toss out the idea that your kiss can change a slimy bastard into a prince because it can't. Pucker up only to kiss him good-bye, if at all.

A toad is an often slick and always slimy lad with a long agenda—one that has nothing to do with having a healthy relationship with you. Whether he's a cheater, liar, abuser, addict, or disrespectful and dismissive idiot, you'll need to cut the codependent cord and move on—no matter how painful or scary change might be.

A toad might make you feel good every so often, but the end of the story is always a culmination of issues, drama, anxiety, frustration, and emotional chaos. Think of it this way: do you want a modern-day fairy tale, or do you want to be stuck in a Lifetime movie?

Now, no maiden goes to the ball with the intention of hooking up with an unavailable lad or a slimy bastard, but unfortunately, there are quite a few out there, and boy, do they clean up nicely! They talk the royal talk and walk the blue-blood walk, and before you know it you're under their spell. It's a spell every maiden has caught herself living under. Somehow these lads know just what to say and do to get us to hop into bed or run circles around them in swollen, blistered heels. But I have some great news for you. You are about to learn the identifying traits of these little creatures, which means you can look forward to a wart-free heart from here to your ever after.

They can be smooth or shady, romantic or repulsive. These creatures are great at deceiving us and even better at getting us to deceive ourselves. If you realize you are dating a toad, you have to toss him back into the pond, no matter how long you have been dealing with him or how many warts you have on your heart. There is no shame in having dated one, but you should always be proud when you recognize it and move on.

See the descriptions that follow to find out if you are dating a toad who has to go.

True Story

I once dated a guy for four years and was certain he was my prince. I adored him, loved him, and treated him like a king. We had even been discussing marriage until one day it came out that he had been cheating on me for three of the four years we had been together. This creep had been with nearly two dozen maidens behind my back! There were twenty-two to be exact. *Twenty-two*, as in ten plus twelve equals EW!

Needless to say, my dreams of a happy ending turned into my worst nightmare all in the course of an evening. My life unraveled over his being caught and subsequent confessions. The craziest part of the story: I stayed another year, trying to forgive him, only to watch my once optimistic and trusting self morph into a suspicious and jealous maiden I never wanted to become. Thankfully, I dumped this loser and six months later found my prince.

While we all might like to believe that a toad can change, most of them never will—at least not for you because they have already betrayed and hurt you. No matter how hard you might try to forgive and forget, the scar will remain. You deserve more, don't you? Of course you do!

He Disrespects You

Disrespect comes in many forms, and all of them should be deal breakers. He might put you down, show up late, embarrass you with nasty comments, or refuse to hold himself accountable for things that make you uncomfortable. He may disrespect your property or treat you like your time, thoughts, or words don't matter. He does this because, in his eyes, they don't. He's an ass. Drop him.

No matter how much you try and explain yourself, teach him, or demand that he treat you better, someone who treats you like this will not change. Either they are threatened by you, are jealous of you, feel a desire to control you, are dealing with their own issues, or are just selfish, insensitive jerks. Whatever the reason, it's his problem and it's too exhausting to stick around and play the "please be nice to me and value me" game. You deserve to be heard, loved, supported, appreciated, and respected—and real love comes with heaping helpings of all of the above.

You want reality? He's an idiot, but you don't have to be the idiot who falls for his promises to change when you threaten to walk. It might be scary to toss a toad back into the pond, especially if you have been with him a while, but every moment you stay with someone who devalues you, you give away a piece of your self-esteem, and, remember, you have earned the right to feel good about yourself.

A real prince is someone who appreciates time with you and places an extremely high value on your intelligence, companionship, time, and words. He lifts you up, encourages you, and makes you feel cherished. Go find him, and drop this loser.

He Has Cheated on You

This guy lives on the defensive and is shady about where he has been; when he answers his phone he always leaves you with the feeling there is a side to him that you don't know about.

If your lad doesn't answer his phone when you are around, has specific rules governing "boys' night out," takes the defensive position when you inquire about strange behavior, or tells you your concerns are based on insecurity and jealousy after you find an earring or answer a hang-up call at his place, look out! A cheating toad doesn't always flaunt his two-timing ways, but he's as busy as a stepsister preparing for the ball when it comes to trying to cover it up. Living a double life isn't easy, and the longer he hops around, the more tired he'll become. This means that unless he's James Bond (and he's not), he'll get sloppy.

If you suspect your guy is cheating on you, don't fly off of the handle until you have solid proof, but don't brush off your concern either. You feel this way for a reason, so even if he is not cheating, there are trust issues you need to discuss. Talk to him, and pay attention to his reaction. Does he understand your concerns, or does he get defensive and angry? Pay close attention to his behavior, watch for significant changes, and always trust your intuition. Does he look you in the eye, or are his eyes darting around? If you have in fact caught your guy cheating, get out fast. This is especially true if he didn't come clean on his own with massive amounts of regret and the solid understanding that it was over, because you deserve better.

No matter how much you love him, a cheater is someone who made a choice to make his selfish desires a bigger priority than your trust. Cheaters put their partner's emotional, physical, and mental health at risk in order to satisfy their own selfish desire for an ego boost or an orgasm. You deserve better—end of story.

Staying stuck in the mud with someone who has betrayed you will not only keep you away from the ball but will have you drowning in a sea of negative emotions such as stress, anxiety, suspicion, and possibly low self-esteem. Your trust matters. Broken promises, betrayal, and disrespect have no place in a healthy relationship.

He Lies to You

Good relationships are based on trust, and once that trust is broken, it's hard to put it back together without noticing the cracks. It might not involve another woman, but if your guy is lying to you about something, being secretive about things, or leaving you with the unsettling feeling you are being kept in the dark, there's a good chance he's got an ulterior motive—and you're on the fast track to getting hurt.

Not only is playing detective no way to spend a relationship, it's no fun and it's exhausting. If you are sharing your life, body, and vulnerabilities with someone, you have the right to know who they are and not have to decode distorted information. If he can't be truthful with the person he's closest to, he has issues that far exceed anything you can fix by loving him. If he lies about one thing, you can bet that's just the lie he was caught in. It takes a lie to cover a lie, and pretty soon you're in a heaping pile of untruths. Get out now.

He Verbally Abuses You

You were completely happy with yourself—until you met your guy. Suddenly, you no longer feel attractive, question your own judgment, and feel like a social outcast. He says he loves you, but it seems as if everything you say and do is wrong. The soles of your feet are bleeding from all of the eggshells you have been walking on!

Your partner may not like everything about you, but that doesn't mean he has the right to tear you down, call you names, or imply that you have an inability to make good decisions about your own life. If your partner is criticizing you, has called you names, has claimed you were "crazy" when you told him how you feel, or always counters you (where he always opposes what you say or tells you what you should do or have done), there is a good chance you are being verbally abused.

The National Domestic Violence Hotline at 1-800-799-SAFE (7233) can offer some helpful advice and help you get any assistance you might need. If he has ever hit you or threatened you harm, please call them and get somewhere safe now. Toads like this do not change, and no one has the right to harm you no matter what you might have done.

No one deserves to be abused, especially by someone who claims to love them. Being attacked and criticized is not love. It's being bullied.

He Is the Dr. Jekyll/Mr. Hyde Toad

He swings from mood to mood faster than you can say, "what the . . . ?" This kind of toad acts like a prince one minute, but say or do the wrong thing and he's making you feel like pond scum in no time. Unless you are into double-dating, drama, and a whole lot of frustration, tell him three's a crowd, and ditch this two-faced reptile!

I'm no therapist, but common sense tells me that dating someone who can't even maintain consistent personality characteristics is not the best bet for a consistent and healthy relationship. Consistency and security are essential components of good, healthy relationships. Besides, how sore are your feet from walking on eggshells?

He Has a Drug/Drinking Problem

Having a cocktail is one thing, but any lad who is drinking heavily or using drugs is self-medicating, and you have to question what emotion or issue is causing him to want to escape reality. It's hard to be a responsible adult when you are tied to an addiction and unable to face your demons.

Addictions control the life of the addict, which means you'll always come in second. You'll have to cope with his erratic behavior, his mood changes, and the bad judgment calls he will inevitably make when he is drunk or high. Also, if he freaks out on you and blames the substance, know that you just got a glimpse of the real him and what he is working so hard to suppress. Nothing good has ever come from alcohol or drugs. You might have a good time, but inevitably there is a downward spiral. Ever watch any of the "E! True Hollywood Stories"?

He's Married/Attached

It doesn't matter what his story is, there is something to be said about a toad who would rather lie and cheat than just be a man and end things. No matter what his excuse is, he is having a relationship with two women, which means he is cheating on his significant other and asking you to play a less significant role in his life. Besides, there's a very good chance he's not telling you the whole story. You deserve someone who is willing to give you 100 percent of his commitment, love, and respect. You deserve to love and respect yourself enough not to play a role in a lie.

Ribbit Tidbits!

Here are some other signs telling you that you need to toss him back.

~ **He has rage issues.** Yelling and screaming, hitting things, and losing it are the signs of an out-of-control person, and people who are not in control are dangerous.
~ **He uses you.** He wants an iPod, so you get him one. He needs a place to stay, so you let him move in. He men-

tions how badly he wants to go to France, so you take him. Meanwhile, he won't even pick up your cold medicine without a fight. Hello?!

~ **He's rude to others.** He might be nice to you, but any lad who's rude to the world has a superiority complex that will inevitably unravel on you as time goes by. Besides, how embarrassing!

~ **He's jealous/controlling.** You are a grown maiden who has achieved a lot in her life, and you are trustworthy and committed. You don't need a warden or a life coach. You need a mate who respects and encourages you!

~ **He's sexist.** Comments that suggest you are weaker, less intelligent, or less capable of doing what he can because you're female is a sign of a reptile who does not respect women. Do you want your children raised by that kind of person?

~ **He plays with your emotions.** He says he feels the same way about you as you do him, so why won't he stop dating other maidens? Because he's selfish and one step away from a cheater—only you are letting him cheat on you in the open.

~ **You get a "bad feeling" about him.** There is a big difference between butterflies in your tummy and an alarm going off in your head. Pay attention, and when the bell rings, find the nearest exit and run for emotional safety!

The Best Songs for Getting a Toad Out of Your System

"I'm Outta Love," Anastasia

"Fighter," Christina Aguilera

"It's Not Right (but It's OK)," Whitney Houston

"Sorry," Madonna

"Believe," Cher

"Sunday Morning," No Doubt

"Ain't That Funny," Jennifer Lopez

"Shake It Off," Mariah Carey

"Stronger," Britney Spears

And, of course . . . "I Will Survive," Gloria Gaynor

(Hey, it works!)

Chapter 11

How and Where to
Bag Your Royal

O K, GALS. IT'S ON. You have really been working on getting to know yourself. You have stopped looking for a man and started looking for a mate. You've dated yourself, and you know and have accepted that Cinderella was a liar. Better yet, you're OK with it and know that you are capable of achieving happiness in spite of her fibs.

You have realized that outside of chocolate and sunsets, there's no such thing as perfect anything—especially when we're talking about human beings. Being the smart maiden you are, you know that every person has a varying amount of flaws and attributes as well as quirks and pet peeves. You are ready to find a guy with whom you share many of these traits in common or whom you are able to accept and for whom you offer (and get) a nice balance. You have tossed Cinderella's tale aside and gotten down to the nitty-gritty; you deserve a big congratulations and something for your efforts. And I have just that something for you!

Are you ready for some good news?

Now that you have stopped looking for a castle to move into, a "perfect" match, a male clone, someone to slay your dragons, or a father figure to care for and protect you, you are finally free to find a solid mate with whom you can create your own happy ending! The world is full of royals who are all interested in meeting a great maiden they can have a good time with and share a part of themselves with. Whether you're looking for a conservative intellectual with a passion for politics or a laid-back surfer type with a dream of traveling the world, rest assured that the lad you are looking for is out there. The problem is we are looking for them in the wrong places. We think our guy doesn't exist because we spend time searching for him in places he would never frequent and waste our time attending the wrong balls!

Now, let's think about this for just a moment. Do you really believe you're going to find a family-oriented homebody at 11:00 P.M. on a Thursday night out at the bars? Girl, please. You know better than that. Who convinced you that the metrosexual clubber would be at the St. Mary's singles mixers? And please, stop with the speed dating! Yuck! You can't possibly think so little of yourself to force yourself to go on thirty-second dates. Speed dating is the CliffsNotes of courtship, and even a realist needs a little romance!

Once you stop following your crazy cousin Nancy out to local clubs and feeling sorry for yourself that you didn't meet your future husband at Bootylicious, you can start attending functions where your particular kind of suitor hangs out. Look at the following profiles to increase your odds of slipping your tootsies in something more comfortable—no magic required!

The Business-Minded Suitor

HIS PEDIGREE: He's conservative, sharp, well-educated, and shrewd in the boardroom. He loves the *Wall Street Journal*, owns several pairs of cuff links, and spends his summers in the Hamptons. This lad cares about his reputation as a conservative Casanova, which is why he'll go to the strip clubs with clients and ogle the double Ds, but in real life he prefers Burberry to bebe.

HIS DEEP DARK SECRET: Whether he's in finance, law, or politics, he didn't get there on those good looks alone. Chances are he spent a lot of time making out with his books. There's a very good chance he's a little bit of a reformed geek who makes his assistant get his overpriced sushi rolls at lunchtime.

HIS KINGDOM: You'll find him shopping at Brooks Brothers and Pink, dining at steak houses and traditional "well-known" establishments, and working out on the elliptical machine on his lunch break. This man loves Starbucks, but don't bother batting those lashes during the 7:00 A.M. rush; he'll be playing with his BlackBerry. A better bet would be striking up a conversation while he waits for his 3:00 P.M. tall, skinny cap.

HIS WEAKNESS: A maiden who wears diamond studs, knows what a coffee press is, and isn't afraid to use it (especially when entertaining his mother).

CONQUER HIM! Log onto Citysearch.com and check out the best places for happy hours that are around banks, law firms, and political offices. These guys are big on cocktails on Thursdays after work. Hotel bars are hot (if you're in New York, L.A., or Miami, you will also meet Metro Prince there), as is the gym between noon and 3:00 P.M.

The Metrosexual Suitor

HIS PEDIGREE: There is no shame in his primping. He's bronzed, smooth, toned, and dressed in the finest threads that he knows will impress. He knows all of the hottest clubs, spends his free time in the gym (checking out his fantastically defined six-pack), and, yes, just might curl his lashes and spray his cologne "down there." Put simply, he's a gay-seeming straight guy, which has its perks. He'll always smell good, have fantastic products for you to sneak when you stay over (his five-hundred-thread-count duvet and goose down pillows are to die for!), and, really, who doesn't love a man who takes you shopping as a day date?

HIS DEEP DARK SECRET: Sure he seems stylin', but that's another word for vain; and in my book, unless you're David Beckham, vanity stems from insecurity. So, what you've got now is an insecure boy who looks like he's in a boy band.

HIS KINGDOM: You'll find him at Fred Segal in L.A., Atrium in New York, and Barneys on both coasts. He wears pink, gets facials, and will sit next to you getting a mani and pedi without the least bit of shame. Strike up a conversation before he goes in for his brow waxing, or pop into the local Hollywood Tans on your lunch hour. Compliment him on his skin/shirt/haircut—hell, on anything—and he'll gladly open up.

HIS WEAKNESS: A maiden who doesn't mind a man with a feminine side and who just might indulge such a side with at-home facials.

CONQUER HIM! He's walking around Soho on the weekends, dining at the trendiest restaurants Wednesday through Saturday, and having drinks at outdoor hotel bars in the summertime (or year-round in warmer locales). Get dressed up in your finest, wax those brows, and get that pedi, because if you want this suitor's slipper, that foot had better be polished and buffed. His big night out is Saturday, and he's at brunch at trendy spots on Sunday around 1:00 P.M.

The Laid-Back "Common" Suitor

HIS PEDIGREE: He might be a royal, but don't expect to be living like a queen anytime soon. This lad would rather order in than order anyone around, and his idea of a romantic night usually involves two dogs and a couple of beers at the game. This blue blood loves blue jeans, baseball caps, and cotton undies with his favorite team's logo.

HIS DEEP DARK SECRET: He's the guy who will show up to your cousin's wedding in a suit he wore in high school. He doesn't understand why you want him to shave, and he'll be damned if he's ever going to step foot in Zara.

HIS KINGDOM: This is the guy who steers clear of swanky clubs but knows the bartenders by name at the local pub. He'll order wings while watching the game on a Sunday afternoon and can be found shopping at the Gap, Old Navy, or his favorite sporting goods store—but only when the clothes in his closet have gotten too ratty to ignore. He likes to relax. Bowling alleys, ball games, pool halls, or places where local bands are playing are all great venues for meeting Mr. Laid-Back. Oh, and the only time he does brunch is when he's hungover—and that is only if the closest diner doesn't deliver.

HIS WEAKNESS: A maiden who doesn't mind beer-pong, drinks beer, plays darts, and looks as cute in a baseball cap and his sweater as she does heels.

CONQUER HIM! It's all about low-maintenance ladies. You had better not be ordering your dressing on the side or be allergic to pizza and dive bars. This suitor is looking for someone who can chill out with him, enjoy life, and not create complicated situations or force him to wear clothes that cost more than his rent.

The Athletic Suitor

HIS PEDIGREE: He's fit, competitive, and healthy. This is the suitor who gets off on the rush of endorphins that comes with a good game, run, or workout—in the gym and between the sheets.

HIS DEEP DARK SECRET: He worries about calories, carbs, and fat, too. A lad who works on his body is acutely aware of weight gain because it shows up so quickly. Expect a lot of grilled chicken in your life.

HIS KINGDOM: He's playing soccer in the park, running by the water in the spring, and working up a sweat in the local gym.

HIS WEAKNESS: A maiden who appreciates her body enough to take good care of it. She will be the woman who can keep up with him at the gym and then run home and slip into a slinky number that shows her perfectly toned legs.

CONQUER HIM! Walk up to him and ask him to show you some new moves, or run next to him and ask him for the time. If you're really ballsy, compliment his arms by telling him they look great, and ask him to show you some moves to help you get that kind of tone.

The Suitor Who Wants a Family

HIS PEDIGREE: He's played the game, sowed his oats, and attended enough balls to last a lifetime. He's comfortable with who he is, and he's ready to share his life with a maiden who is good enough in his eyes to raise his heirs.

HIS DEEP DARK SECRET: He really wants you to meet his mother.

HIS KINGDOM: This lad might still go out for a beer with his buddies, but his clubbing days are over. He's not interested in meeting party girls in their early twenties, and he'd rather play baseball with his little brother than play the field.

HIS WEAKNESS: An understanding and patient maiden with a good head on her shoulders and a nurturing and loving personality.

CONQUER HIM! Show up at Little League games with sandwiches, share stories about your childhood, and invite him over for dinner instead of expecting him to take you out to a trendy restaurant.

The Creative Suitor

HIS PEDIGREE: He's into many different things; he might be in production but also writes, paints, and acts. Creative individuals are usually bursting with new ideas and get bored easily, so there is a good chance he's a jack-of-many-trades.

HIS DEEP DARK SECRET: He can be moody, and he probably doesn't have a lot of money.

HIS KINGDOM: You'll find him at gallery openings, watching independent films, attending movie festivals, in the photography or film section of the bookstore, and in coffee shops. There's a good chance he'll be taking classes—language, writing, photography, painting, or acting classes. He might very well be into yoga or tai chi. These suitors tend to be more open-minded and creative in their pursuits.

HIS WEAKNESS: A maiden who supports his "art" and doesn't push him to work for "the man."

CONQUER HIM! Invite him to an art festival, to a play downtown, or for a drink in a new wine bar or microbrewery—as long as it's different and fun, he's in!

The Suitor Looking for a Good Time

HIS PEDIGREE: You want a no-strings fling, and he's all about it. He is a lot of fun, is not interested in sharing feelings or drama, gives very good cell phone, *and, well, you know . . .*

HIS DEEP DARK SECRET: He really won't get attached, and that condom in his wallet is new.

HIS KINGDOM: He's offering you a drink at clubs, hitting on you in the street, and winking at you at your sister's birthday party. This guy is everywhere; it's up to you to let him know you are down with it.

HIS WEAKNESS: La Perla.

CONQUER HIM! This guy is not hard to conquer because just about every single suitor out there has a bit of him in them. Invite him to your place, and live out whatever fantasies you would like to. Just don't ask him to stay for breakfast (or expect him to).

The Rock 'n' Roll Suitor

HIS PEDIGREE: He loves good bass and wears leather pants without the least bit of irony. He's stylish, sexy, carefree, and having too much fun to worry about a close shave or dropping off his dry cleaning. He might also be the clean-cut finance guy with the obscure piercing or Fender watch. Look for clues, because rock 'n' roll suitors don't always ride Harleys.

HIS DEEP DARK SECRET: He idolizes Bono and secretly performs in front of mirrors when Zeppelin comes on. He wants you to hear his rebel yell and hates people who like Ozzy because of his show on MTV.

HIS KINGDOM: He's watching bands at the hole in the wall on Wednesday nights and playing air guitar in between beers at the dive bar down the street. He's also hounding his assistant to get tickets to Metallica—*for clients, of course.*

His weakness: That tattoo at the nape of your neck that you hide in the office.

Conquer him! Smile at him when he stands next to you in the elevator (you'll be able to recognize him from the loud screeching coming from his iPod). Or casually insert Jerry Cantrell in a conversation. Start humming a little Nirvana or Green Day.

The Guy's Guy Suitor (AKA "the Caveman")

His pedigree: Whether he's attempting to work on his car, playing football, or taking all of his friends down in a drunken arm-wrestling match, the caveman is all about testosterone, sweat, and high fives.

His deep dark secret: He secretly wishes he could have been Braveheart.

His kingdom: He's grunting at the gym and staring in horror at his metrosexual friend who just got his eyebrows waxed. You'll find him in pool halls, at boxing matches, making beer runs, getting too riled up at sporting events, and running across the street to carry your boxes for you because he wants to show you how strong he is.

His weakness: When you wear something frilly and need his help carrying a heavy box.

Conquer him! Challenge him to anything, or compliment him on his ability to burp the alphabet. Offer to take him to Hooters for "beer and wings night," and he might just propose.

Ten Tips for Meeting Suitors

Men love to meet women, and they love it when women show an interest without being too brash or forward. Compliments will make any guy smile, and flashing an inviting smile is enough to make any lad's morning. Here are some tips for the pickup—no cheesy one-liners required.

1. **At the bank or supermarket**—ask him for the time, or borrow a pen. Better yet, ask him to grab something for you on the top shelf.
2. **At a sporting event or watching a game at a bar**—ask him to explain a play or why he likes his favorite team. But never put his team down, even jokingly. (They are extremely sensitive about their sports!) Oh, and never utter the words, "It's just a game." Another tip: make a bet on a play—whoever loses has to buy a round. This will show him you're fun and laid back, and it will appeal to his competitive side.
3. **Online**—send him a smile or a message that is less your life story and more about him such as, "I like your picture; it looks like it was taken on a great day; where were you?"
4. **At a party or social event**—ask him how he knows the host or hosting company. Ask him if he'd like anything from the bar or if he can help you get the DJ to play some old-school Michael Jackson.

5. **At a bar**—ask him what he drinks, and tell him you'll buy him a round if he can tell you something to make you laugh within the next sixty seconds.

6. **Through friends**—tell your friends to hold an impromptu happy hour and introduce you to their cute friend in the picture.

7. **At a restaurant**—while out with your girlfriends, send a round of drinks to a table of guys with an invitation to meet at the bar after dinner. Too forward? Ask him if you should get the filet or salmon.

8. **In a class, marathon, or group situation**—ask to practice, train, or study together.

9. **At a wedding, holiday party, or "couples function"**—send him a smile and, if he's receptive, go over and get his opinion on the band or DJ. Ask him what kind of music he likes (and always mention you like Led Zeppelin, if you do).

10. **Anywhere**—smile and say "hello."

Chapter 12

Real Royals
Answer Questions for You

*A*LL RIGHT LADIES! Are you ready to stop overanalyzing and wondering what he's thinking? Do
you really want to know what happens during those
three-day bachelor parties in Vegas and what will make him
want to commit? Of course you do! You know how I know?
Because you are the ones who sent in the questions! I took all
of the questions sent in by women around the country to hundreds of men from a variety of socioeconomic, religious, and
ethnic backgrounds. Be warned: the quotes you are about to
read range from the surprising to the utterly shocking.

Though some of the responses are a bit disappointing (read
whether they have to like us to sleep with us), the great thing
about these quotes is that all of them are different. Just because
one man cheats doesn't mean they all do, and relax, they don't
want you to be like their mother. Enjoy, ladies!

What is the best age to get married?
"Twenty-eight."

—MIKE, CHICAGO, IL

"When you find the one you love and when you can see your children in her eyes."

—HAROLD, THIRTY-ONE, NEW YORK, NY

"I would say thirty. If for no other reason than because that's the age my dad got married."

—NIKA, THIRTY, KOSOVO

"Thirty-two."

—NICK, THIRTY-THREE, LOS ANGELES, CA

"Another couple of years, no matter what age you are."

—MARTY, THIRTY, LOS ANGELES, CA

"When you can't get laid by anyone else because you have gone bald."

—COREY, TWENTY-NINE, SAN FRANCISCO, CA

What is something a woman can do on a first date that will ruin her chances with you?
"Get drunk. I have ended relationships solely based on the drunken factor. Just maintain and hold your own. But I am 190 pounds; I can drink two bottles of wine. You are half my size, so don't try to keep up; it's not attractive."

—STEVE, THIRTY-THREE, DETROIT, MI

"Dress like a porn star. Nobody wants their girl to dress like a porn star. But it's nice when a woman can exude the same confidence . . . at times."

—LEW, TWENTY-EIGHT, NEW YORK, NY

"Not talk at all."

—STEVE, TWENTY-NINE, CHARLOTTE, NC

"Be a drama queen. Look, we all have our baggage, but I don't need to hear about your two divorces and father who committed suicide on date number one. True story."

—CLIFF, THIRTY-ONE, AUSTIN, TX

"It's hard to say it, but being overly sexually aggressive. Most likely if she's acting like this for me, she's been here before one too many times."

—MARCELLO, TWENTY-NINE, CHICAGO, IL

"Act crazy. She does not have to wield a knife, but overreact, get overemotional, or cling to me, and I'm out of there."

—SAMIT, THIRTY-THREE, SAN FRANCISCO, CA

"Act stupid and silly."

—LES, TWENTY-FOUR, LOS ANGELES, CA

What are some things a woman can do to impress you on a date?
"Offer to pay. I'd never let her in a million years, but the fact that she offers is huge and shows me she's not a gold digger."

—LAYTON, THIRTY-FIVE, HOUSTON, TX

"When two people exchange glances, it's usually up to the guy to make the first move. It's pretty impressive when the woman initiates the conversation."

—NICKEY, TWENTY-TWO, HONOLULU, HI

"Smile, laugh, display joy and enthusiasm (have a sense of humor)."

—CILO, TWENTY-THREE, LONG ISLAND, NY

"Have opinions about a variety of things such as music, art, pop culture, politics, books, and the like."

—LUKE, TWENTY-SEVEN, QUINCY, MA

"Be sincerely interested in what I have to say and/or finding out things about me and be relaxed and cool. This is hard to elaborate on, but don't be the opposite (uptight and too serious). It's a date—not a marriage tryout. This is just two people having a good time."

—TAD, TWENTY-SIX, BRYN MAWR, PA

"Do not sleep with us too soon. Sure, some guys might jump at the chance, but the good ones will always lose respect for you."

—MARK, TWENTY-EIGHT, BALTIMORE, MD

"Be genuine, kind, and outgoing without trying too much."

—JASON, THIRTY-FIVE, ST. PETERSBURG, FL

Share a few secrets about men with women.
"Men want women who are willing to take risks. The cautious women that are 'trying to just not get hurt' rarely get very far."

—RYAN, TWENTY-FOUR, NEW YORK, NY

"If the timing isn't right, neither compatibility nor passion will result in a committed relationship. Men have to be ready, and if a woman speeds up the process and is somehow successful, the man will harbor resentment."

—PETE, THIRTY-FOUR, KANSAS CITY, MO

"They are always children, they need lots of attention, and they need to feel sexy."

—DOMINIC, FORTY-FIVE, PHILADELPHIA, PA

"When I say 'Yes, I'm listening to you honey,' my mind is doing one of three things: (a) reliving great high school sports moments, (b) humming the 'A-Team' theme song, (c) trying to remember the roster of the 1988 New York Yankees."

—BRIAN, TWENTY-SEVEN, NEW YORK, NY

"Here are a few: we love chick flicks, we will read your magazines when you are not around, taking a bath and using your hair and face products is fun (when nobody is around), we are fascinated by breasts, and we want to call more than we do."

—THADD, TWENTY-NINE, GALT, CA

What really happens at bachelor parties?
"Not what you'd think. Yes there are strippers involved in about 65 percent of bachelor parties, but they pretty much just take their clothes off and the guys look at them. That's about it. Some guys get a little carried away with a lap dance, but there is almost never any sex of any kind involved. Drinking? Yes. Drugs? Sure. Naked girls? Yes. Any type of sex, even for the single guys at the bachelor party, no. Bachelor parties are more like funerals than parties. Sex is for birthdays, New Year's, and Easter."

—JUSTIN, THIRTY-ONE, ENCINO, CA

"You don't get to know because then we won't get to have them."

—MARTY, THIRTY-ONE, LOS ANGELES, CA

"I once went to one where we had twenty-five hookers who did a show and then offered favors in the back. Since there were so many, it turned into an orgy basically. I was so amazed by what went on. I did not get involved. I have also been to a bachelor party where we went to Dallas BBQ. . . . I guess it all depends on the crowd. . . . My bachelor party will be joint, with the woman I'm searching to find. We'll gather friends, go to dinner, and get smashed at an Irish pub."

—GUSTAVO, THIRTY-THREE, WAYNE, NJ

"Monopoly, a few sodas, maybe a pickup game of twister."

—LUKE, TWENTY-SEVEN, BOSTON, MA

"Some men cheat. Actually, most of the time there is a guy in the group who cheats and makes a fool out of himself, but the rest of us are usually staring at him in disgust and talking about him behind his back. There is usually a steak house, some strippers, some big talking, pathetic late-night calls to our wives and girlfriends, and gambling guilt."

—STEVE, THIRTY-FIVE, DALLAS, TX

"I know at mine one of the strippers had BO."

—CHARLIE, TWENTY-EIGHT, LOS ANGELES, CA

Do all men cheat? What will make a man cheat?
"Absolutely not. This is a bad stereotype. If I'm in a happy relationship, I'll forgo any opportunity to cheat, and I have a lot of them because of my job where I'd never get caught. I'm out

of town a lot in social situations. But it's not about getting 'caught'; it's about having the respect for the girlfriend/wife. If I'm to the point where I'm truly tempted, it's probably not going to work out."

—IAN, THIRTY-ONE, AUSTIN, TX

"Not all men, just boys. Someone who knows how hurtful that is would never do that to someone else. Men know this; boys don't!"

—BOBBY, THIRTY-ONE, LOS ANGELES, CA

"Yes. Their penis."

—KRIS, TWENTY-EIGHT, NEW YORK, NY

"No, not all. It depends on what stage in life they are in. If a man doesn't really know who he is yet or what he wants, then he'll probably cheat. Also, booze is a good catalyst. Lots of booze. Oh, and drugs too. Or being in a band. Or famous at all. And if they have a lot of money. Or if they have a penis. Yes, all men probably cheat at some point in their lives."

—DAVID, TWENTY-SEVEN, BOSTON, MA

"Depends on your definition; if cheating is having 'thoughts' of being with another woman, like a fantasy, then without question all men cheat. If flirting with another woman, even though your intentions may not be there, then yes, all men cheat. If it's physical, then no."

—CRAIG, TWENTY-NINE, CHICAGO, IL

"No, we do not all cheat. I have never cheated and never plan on cheating."

—WESLEY, TWENTY-NINE, ROYERSFORD, PA

"I for one could not imagine doing that to my wife. It is not so much the act but the hurt it would provoke in the person I love the most. The act itself is selfish; after you commit yourself to someone this sort of self-centeredness should be left behind."

—ANTHONY, TWENTY-EIGHT, CHICAGO, IL

Will you date a woman long term if you have no intention of marrying her?
"Yes . . . I know personally I have dated women that were fun but not the type you marry. Sometimes it just sucks to be alone so you settle for a not-so-perfect girlfriend."

—DRAKER, THIRTY-FOUR, BROOKLYN, NY

"Depends on where I am in my life."

—ROBERT, THIRTY-TWO, NEW YORK, NY

"No, there is no point if you know at some time down the line you are both going to be hurt very bad as a result of the situation. However, it's impossible to know who you are going to marry unless you date someone long term, so a better question to ask is can you see yourself dating this person for ten years instead of do I want to marry this person?"

—JUSTIN, TWENTY-SIX, NEWARK, DE

"Yes. Men will string women along for good sex."

—HARRY, TWENTY-NINE, BETHESDA, MD

Is there a connection between sex and love?
"Yes there is. Men love sex."

—KRIS, TWENTY-EIGHT, NEW YORK, NY

"I'm still trying to figure that one out."

—ROBERTO, TWENTY-FIVE, BROOKLYN, NY

"Yes and no. Sex is more like screwing, whereas love is like when you make love. There is a difference that is kinda indescribable, but everyone knows when you are having sex or making love. You can make love at night then the next morning have sex."

—LEROY, THIRTY, ROYERSFORD, PA

"There does not have to be, but it's nicer when there is."

—JACK, FORTY-FIVE, PHILADELPHIA, PA

"They're close but different. Depends on what mood you're in. And whether you drank that evening . . . and what you drank . . . and how much you drank . . . and . . . no, that's it."

—LEO, TWENTY-SEVEN, NEW YORK, NY

What are you looking for in a wife? Is it different from a girlfriend?
"Shouldn't be."

—ELTON, TWENTY-SEVEN, NEW YORK, NY

"I will date blondes but marry a brunette . . . just kidding. I just want a woman to be my best friend and someone who will take care of me and I can take care of her."

—TYSON, TWENTY-FOUR, BOSTON, MA

"I don't think what most men look for in a wife and a serious girlfriend is different (probably is different from what would be acceptable for a casual relationship). Men want someone who treats them with respect and genuinely cares about them (learned this is really the most important thing), has a decent sense of humor, is reasonably bright, reasonably ambitious, takes care of herself, has a sense of class/decorum, is confident but not arrogant, has similar interests but also her own mind, cares about what is right, and to whom they are attracted and sexually compatible."

—ALEJANDRO, THIRTY, CHICAGO, IL

"In college, yes. In your thirties, not unless you're an idiot."

—ALEX, THIRTY-TWO, ENCINO, CA

Whoops! We slept with you too soon and now regret it. What do we do?
"Nope, too late."

—GREG, TWENTY-SEVEN, NEW YORK, NY

"Well, this is one factor in determining whether the relationship can ultimately work out or not. For some men, there is probably nothing a woman could do if the man thinks she slept with him too soon. For others, it probably comes down to the woman just continuing to be an attractive person (in the more general sense, not the specific) to the man—someone that he would still want to be in a relationship with. There isn't really a single way of obtaining "redemption"; it is more about showing that she is right for the guy, a quality person. Chances are, if a woman makes a concerted effort to address this concern, specifically, it will backfire. And some guys just aren't going to be able to get past this, no matter what. Move on."

—STEVE, FORTY, WOODBURY, MN

"I know it sounds old-fashioned, but it's just the way it is. I can really like a woman, but if she sleeps with me on the first date, she has ruined it for me; I will just want her out of my life."

—HAROLD, THIRTY-ONE, NEW YORK, NY

Why do men change six months into the relationship?

"Men start to become comfortable. Chris Rock has a famous saying: 'When you are on the first date you are not meeting the person, you are meeting their REPRESENTATIVE. They were sent to say the right things and act the right way, so you like them.' This rings true because everyone puts his best foot forward before he can start letting some things go, because at that point he knows you like him for him. If you lose the romance in six months, then good luck with marriage, because losing interest or romance in six months shows a lack of stability in the relationship."

—HENRY, TWENTY-SEVEN, GREAT NECK, NY

"Because you keep saying it and saying it and saying it."

—GOSOVO, TWENTY-SEVEN, WASHINGTON, DC

"We start out trying not to bore you, and you wind up boring us."

—MIKE, FORTY-SEVEN, PHILADELPHIA, PA

"It's like a two-term president. We do and say all the right things to get elected into a relationship. We work hard to make sure you love us and are happy and content in the relationship. Then once we're certain you can't live without us—that's the second term—we can relax. It's just like a lame-duck president. We become lame-duck guys, lazy and not really listening to you as closely anymore or being as romantic because we don't have to. We're not running for reelection. We're in there."

—BENNY, FIFTY-ONE, LOS ANGELES, CA

What should all women stop doing right now?
"Stop stringing guys along. I would much prefer the straight-up slap in the face than the kick in the groin a few months later."

—VIC, TWENTY-NINE, ROYERSFORD, PA

"Stop analyzing everything."

—HAROLD, THIRTY-ONE, NEW YORK, NY

"Women should stop taking so many things personally. I understand that women are, generally, more emotional than men, but it becomes very frustrating when something is said or done that is in no way meant to be mean and the female takes it to heart. We then have to spend/waste an hour trying to talk ourselves out of it. Most guys don't play dating games and will be forward about any problem they have. I do believe that most of the reason why this happens is I think women read into men's actions a lot more than vice versa."

—COREY, TWENTY-THREE, MANHATTAN BEACH, CA

"Stop worrying about what everyone thinks and feels; do what you want to do and be happy."

—RICKY, THIRTY-THREE, MEXICO CITY, MEXICO

Do you like to cuddle after sex?
"Depends on room temperature. But usually, yes, for a little while."

—TODD, TWENTY-SEVEN, NEW YORK, NY

"We need some time to cool off, literally. Then, if everyone is still awake, sure."

—MIKE, THIRTY-ONE, LOS ANGELES, CA

"Occasionally (first few times, if it is meaningful—which by the way is a pretty good way for a woman to tell what the man's emotional level is), but not for very long—it's just not very physically comfortable."

—JOEY, FORTY, DALLAS, TX

How do we scare you away?
"Making yourself too available too soon."

—WENTWORTH, TWENTY-SEVEN, GREAT NECK, NY

"You can scare us away by appearing too needy, especially early on in the relationship. If we're on our first date and you talk about how you can't wait to get married and have lots of children, chances are excellent that we'll not only not ask you out again, but we'll change our phone number and perhaps even move to another city. Your photo will also be posted on secret websites that men have to warn us about women like you."

—MARK, FIFTY-FIVE, LOS ANGELES, CA

"Being co-dependent. A man wants a woman with a life."

—JASON, THIRTY-SEVEN, BOSTON, MA

What quality do you find least attractive in a woman and why?
"Women should stop being so envious of other women. Women are so concerned with 'keeping up with the Joneses' that it gets

a bit ridiculous. So she lost weight, got a great job, married a good-looking, rich guy; please be happy for each other."

—LEWIS, TWENTY-NINE, GREAT NECK, NY

"Insanity—see dictionary for explanation."

—VANCE, FIFTY-ONE, LOS ANGELES, CA

"Snootiness . . . not sure if that's a word. Basically I hate chicks that gotta have that five hundred–dollar purse. It is a freaking purse!!!! I think it is unattractive when women act all snooty toward other women."

—NOAH, TWENTY-NINE, ROYERSFORD, PA

"Being a doormat. Call me out when I am being an asshole."

—STEVEN, FORTY, WASHINGTON, DC

Why do you take our phone numbers if you have no intention of calling us?
"So we don't embarrass anyone."

—ANTONIO, FORTY, PHILADELPHIA, PA

"To end the conversation amicably."

—PHILLIP, THIRTY-ONE, LOS ANGELES, CA

"It's polite, and we have no balls."

—HENRY, THIRTY-FOUR, NEW YORK, NY

Porn—what's the deal? Do you want us to act like these women?
"No—those women are our fantasy. Our fantasy and reality cannot be one and the same—life would be boring."

—BLAKE, TWENTY-SEVEN, SILVER SPRINGS, MD

"Definitely not in public, but we definitely want them to know what they are doing in bed. If a woman acts like a porn star in bed too soon though, it will scare a man away. It's best if she gets better in the relationship so that we know she's not a slut, because no man wants to be with a slut. We want a great girl who is only a slut in private with us."

—HAROLD, THIRTY-ONE, NEW YORK, NY

"We want you to want to watch it with us and get as turned on by those women."

—JOSHUA, TWENTY-SEVEN, MIAMI, FL

Do you want a nice girl or bitch?
"We want a nice girl, as long as there's just a touch of bitch in there somewhere. If she's too nice, she'll get walked over. If she's too bitchy, no one will want to get near her."

—JOAQUIN, THIRTY-FIVE, LOS ANGELES, CA

"Nice girl. Hate—and I mean HATE—bitchy girls."

—STEPHANO, TWENTY-SEVEN, BROOKLYN, NY

"Not a bitch but nasty at the right times."

—ENRIQUE, THIRTY-SEVEN, SACRAMENTO, CA

Do we analyze too much?
"The fact that you ask is your answer."

—CHARLES, TWENTY-SEVEN, BOSTON, MA

"Sometimes. You should overthink that question and get back to me."

—DEREK, THIRTY, BROOKLYN, NY

"Yes. Ya see, now you're analyzing my answer of 'yes.' It never ends!"

—MARK, TWENTY-SEVEN, NEW YORK, NY

"I'd say most women do. Most men are not out to trick you; you tend to trick yourselves into thinking there is some reason for his not calling or not showing you interest when the reality is, he's not interested."

—HAROLD, THIRTY-ONE, NEW YORK, NY

"Enough to make us hate you a little."

—MIKE, TWENTY-NINE, CHICAGO, IL

Do you fantasize about other women while having sex with us?
"Yes."

—NICK, THIRTY-THREE, HOLLYWOOD, FL

"Not really. That is why it is great to keep the lights on; you don't have to visualize then."

—JASON, THIRTY-ONE, NEW YORK, NY

"Extremely rare. Usually happens when we are regretting hooking up with a girl in the first place."

—STU, TWENTY-SEVEN, NEW YORK, NY

"Not a lot, but if Rebecca Romijn is on the wall . . ."

—NOAH, THIRTY, LOS ANGELES, CA

Do men really fear commitment?
"No—they fear emasculation and a change of lifestyle."

—BENJAMIN, TWENTY-EIGHT, NEW YORK, NY

"Why fear something that will make you happy? They fear committing to the wrong job, the wrong three-course menu at a nice dinner, and the wrong woman."

—HENRY, THIRTY-TWO, TRENTON, NJ

"If he's fearing it, she's not the right woman."

—J.R., THIRTY-TWO, HARTFORD, CT

"This is almost an urban myth. Some men do and some don't. Some women are obsessed with shoes, some aren't."

—PETER, THIRTY-SIX, SHREVEPORT, LA

What does a man need to figure out in his life before he's ready to settle down with one woman?
"If she can be a good mommy."

—AL, TWENTY-NINE, NEW YORK, NY

"That he has the room in his heart to love her, the money in the bank to support her, and the self-control to honor his promise to remain faithful to her."

—TONY, THIRTY-FIVE, LAS VEGAS, NV

"There is just a day when you wake up and you have had enough of the party life and are ready. It's kind of like that lady that said, 'Men are like taxicabs when their light goes on; they take the first passenger they see.' "

—FRED, THIRTY, SAN FRANCISCO, CA

"That he has failed at being able to get sex without getting married."

—MIKE, TWENTY-EIGHT, LOS ANGELES, CA

"Most basically, he needs to figure out what he wants in a woman, and he needs to figure out what is realistic in terms of expectations. This doesn't mean that he has to be ready/willing to 'settle,' but just that he has to realize not filling the ice trays or thinking *Fletch* is the greatest movie ever shouldn't be a 'deal breaker'—a perfect match is not a mirror image, and there is no one who won't occasionally annoy you. Essentially, a man must want to be happy, be able to achieve that himself, and then want to share it with someone who enhances his happiness and is in a similar place."

—ALVIN, FORTY, WASHINGTON, DC

What will make you commit to a woman?

"Someone who I know I will never get bored with or tired of and shows that she is trustworthy."

—JOHN, TWENTY-FOUR, GAITHERSBURG, MD

"Something about her."

—FERNANDO, THIRTY-NINE, NICARAGUA

"I will commit when the time feels right, but that time comes fairly soon. A man does not need a year to figure out if he can be exclusive with a woman."

—STEVEN, THIRTY-EIGHT, PORTLAND, OR

"Men will commit to a woman who is too perfect for him to leave on the market. Men are competitive; if he's serious about you, he'll scoop you up sooner rather than later. Keeping his options open means he does not value you enough."

—VINNY, THIRTY-SIX, SEATTLE, WA

Why do men try and "fix" everything?
"Because we're usually the ones who broke whatever it is that needs to be fixed."

—RICK, TWENTY-FIVE, SAN JOSE, CA

"Why do you break everything?"

—ELIJAH, THIRTY-FOUR, NEWPORT, RI

"Because it's us against the problem, and we have to win so you will think we are the brilliant creatures we wish we were."

—RAHIT, THIRTY-THREE, LOS ANGELES, CA

"It's how we're wired. We can't really help it, although at some point we might become aware of this and try not to do it as much."

—ASHTON, FORTY, SAN FRANCISCO, CA

Do you have to like a girl to sleep with her?
"No, but I do have to like her to let her stay the night."

—JASON, THIRTY-ONE, ENCINO, CA

"The second time, definitely."

—LES, TWENTY-SEVEN, NEW YORK, NY

"Absolutely not. In fact, women don't realize that a guy can HATE you and still sleep with you."

—WILLIAM, TWENTY-SEVEN, BROOKLYN, NY

"Nope. Most of the time we don't, which is why we don't date them."

—ERIK, TWENTY-EIGHT, AUBURN, CA

When a woman is out with a guy, are there any signs she can look for to gauge whether he's interested in a relationship or just a good time?

"Guys are always looking for a good time; relationships develop if she turns out to be great. Always assume he's dating someone else unless you've had a talk about exclusivity. Also, is he treating you like he would want his daughter to be treated? That's a good indication of intent and respect."

—JESSE, THIRTY, NEW YORK, NY

"Yeah, if he invites you to dinner and makes weekend plans with you, he's interested. If he's calling you to meet up with him and his friends or asking you to meet him after he goes out with his friends, he wants to sleep with you. Girls crack me up with this. How can a man be any more obvious than 'wanna come over and sleep with me and be gone in the morning?' "

—ARMAND, THIRTY-FIVE, NORWALK, CT

"Does he want to spend time with you? Does he remember things about you? Does he introduce you to the people in his life? Basic common sense here."

—BARON, TWENTY-EIGHT, AUSTIN, TX

If there were no societal judgments or expectations, would you choose to be monogamous?

"No."

—CIRO, TWENTY-SEVEN, WASHINGTON, DC

"Probably not."

—NICK, FORTY-FIVE, BIG RAPIDS, MI

"Yes. Monogamy is a behavior that is a result of the feelings you hold toward the person you love; it is an effect of the cause; when you love someone you don't want to be with someone else."

— GREG, THIRTY-ONE, SANDY, UT

Are men really as superficial as we think you are?
"I find that to be an offensive generalization that—hey, a girl just walked by outside my window and the wind blew her skirt up and I saw her G-string and everything!"

— VICTOR, FIFTY, PALO ALTO, CA

"No. Simple but not superficial."

— PETE, THIRTY-ONE, LOS ANGELES, CA

"Some people are superficial and some are not, but do all men enjoy looking at a pretty woman? Yes."

— MICHAEL, FIFTY, WASHINGTON, DC

Do you want a woman who is like your mother?
"No, I want a woman who likes my mother."

— STEVE, THIRTY-THREE, NEW YORK, NY

"I'm trying to top my mother; maybe that's why I'm still single."

— ANDREW, TWENTY-SEVEN, QUEENS, NY

"This is so old school. I want someone who is kind and respectful."

— MIKE, FORTY-FIVE, KANSAS CITY, MO

"I want a woman who likes me, likes my mother, and my mother likes her."

—EWAN, FORTY-TWO, MIAMI, FL

The truth about the ring: pleasure or pure obligation?
"Pleasure; I want to give my girl something that makes her feel special and something that she can brag to her friends who get jealous over it. It's the way to start what is supposed to be the most special occasion in your lifetime; of course you should go completely over the top."

—SUDAR, TWENTY-SEVEN, KANSAS CITY, MO

"Pleasure; only a fool does it out of obligation."

—JEREMY, THIRTY-ONE, CHARLOTTE, NC

Your Very Own Coat of Arms

NOW THAT YOU have uncovered the truth, it's time to work on a little something to remind you of all of the things you have learned about yourself, men, and dating. Take out your fanciest pen and get comfy, because it's time to make your very own *Cinderella Was a Liar* coat of arms! (See page 243.)

At the bottom write the phrase that best describes what you are looking for in a partnership. It could be your favorite quote or something as simple as "Respect." Whatever it is, make sure it summarizes your desires and is unique to you. Then, in each of the four sections, I want you to write words and draw pictures that best describe the following four areas.

1. **Your many talents and positive qualities:** Draw your gorgeous almond-shaped eyes, your big heart, or a paintbrush to represent you're in an art class. It's time to remind yourself of the good stuff for a change!

2. **Your step habits:** Put words and symbols in the next box to serve as small reminders of the habits you are trying to break.

3. **Toad repellant:** Whether it's a wallet in a safe to signify a cheapskate, a frown to symbolize negativity, or a nasty word to remind you to be on the lookout for a disrespectful toad, give yourself reminders of your deal breakers, and maintain those boundaries!

4. **Your sweet life:** Write down reminders of all of the blessings, experiences, and positive things in your life that make each day worth celebrating (and have nothing to do with a man)!

Index

About the Author

———•———

BRENDA DELLA CASA contributes regularly to *For Me* magazine and is the only featured female writer on the well-known comedy site thephatphree.com. Brenda has written for *Woman's Day*, *Play Magazine*, *28th Street*, *The Eagle*, and for a variety of online companies and publications.

In addition to her writing experience, Brenda is also an accomplished reality casting agent who has recruited for and cast some of the most popular dating, relationship, and family shows on television.

Once homeless and without a family, Brenda went from scouring the backs of restaurants and fraternity houses for food to attending The American University, where she graduated with a degree in print journalism. While in Washington, DC, Brenda was introduced to her idol, President William Jefferson Clinton, who invited her to the White House. Brenda was granted an internship in the communications office for the following year.

Brenda currently lives and writes in Manhattan with her Prince and her Chihuahua, Tony Montana.